COMMON ENGLISH MISTAKES EXPLAINED WITH EXAMPLES

Over 600 Mistakes Almost Students Make and How To Avoid Them In Less Than 5 Minutes A Day

RACHEL MITCHELL

ISBN: 9781521410967

TABLE OF CONTENT

INTRODUCTION

English mistakes are the things most learners make in study and practice. Learning the most typical mistakes may help students build considerable confidence, become error-free, and successful in using English.

The book is well designed and written by an experienced teacher who has been teaching English for more than 20 years to make sure that all the mistakes inside are the most typical and useful for students at each level.

As the author of this book, I believe that this book will be an indispensable reference and trusted guide for you who may want to learn from the most common mistakes in English vocabulary and grammar, so they could use English in a correct but natural way. Once you read this book, I guarantee you that you will have learned an extraordinarily wide range of useful, and practical English mistakes that will help you become a successful English learner, particularly in examinations such as Cambridge FCE, CAE, CPE, and IELTS; as well as you will even become a successful English user in work and in life within a short period of time only.

Thank you for downloading the book *"Common English Mistakes Explained With Examples: Over 600 Mistakes Almost Students Make and How To Avoid Them In Less Than 5 Minutes A."*

Let's get started!

OVER TOP 600 MISTAKES ALMOST STUDENTS MAKE AND HOW TO AVOID THEM

We say plenty of + noun, (NOT ~~plenty + noun~~).

We have plenty of time to eat. *(Don't say: We have plenty of time to eat).*

He had plenty of chances to apologize, but he didn't. *(Don't say: He had ~~plenty chances~~ to apologize, but he didn't).*

We have plenty of chances to have fun and learn together. *(Don't say: We have ~~plenty chances~~ to have fun and learn together).*

We say a lot of/lots of + noun, (NOT ~~a~~ lots of + noun).

There are a lot of food and fruit in the supermarket. *(Don't say: There are ~~a lots of~~ food and fruit in the supermarket).*

There are lots of people waiting outside. *(Don't say: There are ~~a lots of~~ people waiting outside).*

There are a lot of people at the party. *(Don't say: There are ~~a lots of~~ people at the party).*

We use a great deal of + uncountable nouns, (NOT a great deal of ~~+ countable nouns~~).

She offered me a great deal of money.

He has a great deal of experience.

We use a large amount of + uncountable nouns, (NOT a large amount of ~~+ countable nouns~~).

I lent him a large amount of money.

I feed a large amount of food to my dog.

We use the majority of + plural countable nouns, (NOT the majority of ~~+ uncountable/singular nouns~~).

The majority of students are female. *(Don't say: The majority of ~~student~~ are female).*

The majority of patients are women. *(Don't say: The majority of ~~patient~~ are women).*

We say talk/speak loudly, (NOT talk/speak ~~aloud~~).

He spoke very loudly. *(Don't say: He spoke very ~~aloud~~).*

She talked so loudly that I couldn't hear. *(Don't say: She talked so ~~aloud~~ that I couldn't hear).*

We say read aloud, (NOT read ~~loudly~~).

She read the letter aloud to the rest of the family. *(Don't say: She read the letter ~~loudly~~ to the rest of the family).*

Read the essay aloud to yourself. *(Don't say: Read the essay ~~loudly~~ to yourself).*

We use need + to infinitive, (NOT need + ~~Vo~~).

I need to study hard for the exam. *(Don't say: I need study hard for the exam.).*

She needs to see the doctor. *(Don't say: She needs see the doctor).*

We use need + V-ing or need to be + V3 with the passive form, (NOT need + ~~to infinitive~~).

The house needs painting/to be painted. *(Don't say: The house needs ~~to paint~~).*

My car needs washing/to be washed. *(Don't say: My car needs ~~to wash~~).*

We say no longer, (NOT ~~not longer~~).

She no longer loves him. *(Don't say: She ~~not longer~~ loves him).*

I no longer cook at home. *(Don't say: I ~~not longer~~ cook at home).*

He no longer lives with his parents. *(Don't say: He ~~not longer~~ lives with his parents).*

We say not…any longer or not…any more, (NOT ~~not….no longer~~).

He doesn't play the guitar any longer. *(Don't say: He doesn't play the guitar no longer).*

She doesn't live in Canada any longer. *(Don't say: She doesn't live in Canada no longer).*

She doesn't love me any more. *(Don't say: She doesn't love me no longer).*

She doesn't hang out with me on weekends any more. *(Don't say: She doesn't hang out with me on weekends no longer).*

We say a piece of paper, (NOT a paper or a paper piece).

Give me a piece of paper. *(Don't say: Give me a paper/ a paper piece).*

Write this word down on a piece of paper. *(Don't say: Write this word down on a paper/ a paper piece).*

We use the noun + noun structure to talk about parts of things, (NOT noun + 's + noun).

A house roof. *(Don't say: A house's roof).*

A car door. *(Don't say: a car's door)*

We say a fraction + plural nouns + plural verb or a fraction + singular nouns + singular verb.

Three quarters of the students are girls. *(Don't say: Three quarters of the students is girls).*

Two third of the work has been finished. *(Don't say: Two third of the work have been finished).*

In the front of means inside something.

In front of means outside something.

If you sit in the front of the car, you'll have a better view. *(Don't say: If you sit in front of the car, you'll have a better view).*

He sat in the front of the bus. *(Don't say: He sat in front of the bus).*

We're standing in front of your house. *(Don't say: We're standing ~~in the front of~~ your house).*

We parked our cars in front of the hotel. *(Don't say: We parked our cars ~~in the front of~~ the hotel).*

We say ought to, (NOT ~~oughts to~~).

I think she ought to call the police. *(Don't say: I think she ~~oughts~~ to call the police).*

He ought to drink more water. *(Don't say: He ~~oughts~~ to drink more water).*

He ought to quit smoking. *(Don't say: He ~~oughts~~ to quit smoking).*

We say ought not to + verb, (NOT ~~ought to not + verb~~).

He said that he ought not to waste his time. *(Don't say: He said that he ~~ought to not~~ waste his time).*

You ought not to eat so much chocolate. *(Don't say: You ~~ought to not~~ eat so much chocolate).*

We don't use progressive forms with the verb "believe"

I believed that she would keep her promise. *(Don't say: I ~~was believing~~ that she would keep her promise).*

She believed that he was honest. *(Don't say: She ~~was believing~~ that he was honest).*

We say the man who lives, (NOT the man who ~~he~~ lives).

The man who lives next door to me is a lawyer. *(Don't say: The man who ~~he~~ lives next door to me is a lawyer).*

Do you know the woman who is talking to Peter? *(Don't say: Do you know the woman who ~~she~~ is talking to Peter?).*

We say depend on, (NOT depend ~~of/in~~).

Tom still financially depends on his parents. *(Don't say: Tom still financially depends ~~of/in~~ his parents).*

She has used up her savings and has to depend on her brother to help her out. *(Don't say: She has used up her savings and has to depend off/in her brother to help her out).*

We say from my point of view, (NOT ~~according to~~ my point of view).

From my point of view, America is the most powerful country in the world. *(Don't say: ~~According to~~ my point of view, America is the most powerful country in the world).*

From her point of view, the homeless people are lazy. *(Don't say: ~~According to~~ her point of view, the homeless people are lazy).*

In the end means finally/ after a long period of time.

At the end means the last part of a period of time when something stops.

He worked hard, and in the end, he achieved his goal. *(Don't say: He worked hard, and ~~at~~ the end, he achieved his goal).*

In the end, she voted for him. *(Don't say: ~~At~~ the end, she voted for him).*

Was the film happy at the end? *(Don't say: Was the film happy ~~in~~ the end?).*

No one was happy at the end of the movie. *(Don't say: No one was happy ~~in~~ the end of the movie).*

We say in pen/pencil, (NOT ~~with~~ pen/pencil).

She signed her name in pen. *(Don't say: She signed her name ~~with~~ pen).*

Please write your name in pen. *(Don't say: Please write your name ~~with~~ pen).*

He wrote his name in pencil. *(Don't say: He wrote his name ~~with~~ pencil).*

We say in a picture/photo, (NOT ~~on~~ a picture/photo).

The boat in my picture is 6 inches long. *(Don't say: The boat ~~on~~ my picture is 6 inches long).*

He wrote the names of the animals in his picture. *(Don't say: He wrote the names of the animals ~~on~~ his picture).*

Lucy looks very pretty in her photo. *(Don't say: Lucy looks very pretty on her photo).*

We say in the rain/snow, (NOT under the rain/snow).

We were caught in the rain and got soaked to the skin. *(Don't say: We were caught under the rain and got soaked to the skin).*

When he was walking home from work, he got caught in the rain. *(Don't say: When he was walking home from work, he got caught under the rain).*

We got lost in the snow. *(Don't say: We got lost under the snow).*

I took a walk in the snow. *(Don't say: I took a walk under the snow).*

We don't use prepositions before "next", "last", "this", "that".

He will throw a party next week. *(Don't say: He will throw a party on next week).*

I started my new job last week. *(Don't say: I started my new job on last week).*

I have been very busy this week. *(Don't say: I have been very busy on this week).*

We walked eleven miles that day. *(Don't say: We walked eleven miles on that day).*

We say with whom, (NOT whom.... with).

With whom did you go to the movies? *(Don't say: whom did you go to the movies with?).*

With whom did you go to the concert? *(Don't say: whom did you go to the concert with?).*

We use the present perfect progressive: Have/has + been + V-ing, (NOT Have/has + been + V3/V-ed).

We have been travelling since last September. *(Don't say: We have been travelled since last September).*

My sister has been studying Japanese since 2005. *(Don't say: My sister has been studied Japanese since 2005).*

We use though/although + clause 1, clause 2, (NOT though/although +

clause 1, ~~but~~ clause 2).

Although he really hates grammar, it's useful. *(Don't say: Although he really hates grammar, ~~but~~ it's useful).*

Though she was late, she stopped to buy a sandwich. *(Don't say: Though she was late, ~~but~~ she stopped to buy a sandwich).*

We use since/because + clause 1, clause 2, (NOT since/because + clause 1, ~~so~~ clause 2).

Since/because he was sick, he went to see a doctor. *(Don't say: Since/because he was sick, ~~so~~ he went to see a doctor).*

Since/because she was late, she missed the train. *(Don't say: Since/because she was late, ~~so~~ she missed the train).*

Cattle is a plural noun; it has no singular forms.

Many cattle are sold and exported. *(Don't say: Many ~~cattles~~ are sold and exported).*

Three cattle are getting sick. *(Don't say: Three cattle ~~is~~ getting sick).*

We say the police + plural verb, (NOT the police + ~~singular verb~~).

The police are trying to stop speeding in the city. *(Don't say: The police ~~is~~ trying to stop speeding in the city).*

The police are looking for the robber. *(Don't say: The police ~~is~~ looking for the robber).*

We say the staff + plural verb, (NOT the staff + ~~singular verb~~).

The staff are not very satisfied with the latest pay increase. *(Don't say: The staff ~~is~~ not very satisfied with the latest pay increase).*

The staff are very helpful. *(Don't say: The staff ~~is~~ very helpful).*

The staff are working late. *(Don't say: The staff ~~is~~ working late).*

We say more than one person + singular verb, (NOT more than one person + ~~plural verb~~).

More than one person is aware of the event. *(Don't say: More than one person are aware of the event)*.

More than one person is leaving you. *(Don't say: More than one person are leaving you)*.

We use smell + adjective, (NOT smell + ~~adverb~~).

These roses aren't beautiful, but they smell nice. *(Don't say: These roses aren't beautiful, but they smell nicely)*.

The hamburgers smell delicious. *(Don't say: The hamburgers smell deliciously)*.

We use wish + to infinitive, (NOT wish + ~~V-ing~~).

I wish to go to Hawaii. *(Don't say: I wish going to Hawaii)*.

She wishes to visit her grandmother in the summer. *(Don't say: She wishes visiting her grandmother in the summer)*.

We use be worth + V-ing, (NOT wish + ~~To infinitive~~).

The book is worth reading. *(Don't say: The book is worth to read)*.

This movie is worth watching. *(Don't say: This movie is worth to watch)*.

We say spend time, (NOT ~~pass~~ time).

We spent two weeks in Moscow. It was very fun. *(Don't say: we passed two weeks)*.

Last night he spent two hours writing his essay. *(Don't say: He passed two hours writing his essay)*.

We say spend money, (NOT ~~use~~ money).

If I buy a big house, I'll have to spend a lot of money. *(Don't say: ...I'll have to use a lot of money)*.

He spent a lot of money on drugs and women. *(Don't say: He passed a lot of money on drugs and women)*.

We say International food/cuisine, (NOT ~~worldwide~~ food/cuisine).

International food is becoming popular in many countries. *(Don't say: ~~worldwide~~ food is becoming popular in many countries).*

The restaurant offers local and international cuisine. *(Don't say: The restaurant offers local and ~~worldwide~~ cuisine).*

We say Chinese/ Italian/French food. (NOT ~~China/ Italy/ France~~ food).

I love Chinese food. *(Don't say: I love ~~China~~ food).*

Lucy loves French food. *(Don't say: Lucy loves ~~France~~ food).*

We say do or play sport. (NOT ~~make~~ sport).

I do sport every evening. *(Don't say: I ~~make~~ sport every evening).*

She likes to play sport. *(Don't say: She likes to ~~make~~ sport).*

We say do exercises. (NOT ~~make~~ exercises)

I do exercises every day after work. *(Don't say: I ~~make~~ exercises every day after work).*

My father used to do exercises every day before work. *(Don't say: My father used to ~~make~~ exercises every day before work).*

We say play games. (NOT ~~do~~ games)

He usually plays computer games at the weekend. *(Don't say: He usually ~~does~~ computer games at the weekend).*

The children are playing games. *(Don't say: The children are ~~doing~~ games).*

We say go skiing. (NOT ~~make~~ skiing)

We are planning to go skiing this winter. *(Don't say: We are planning to ~~make~~ skiing this winter).*

I used to go skiing in the winter. *(Don't say: I used to ~~make~~ skiing in the winter).*

We say do activities. (NOT ~~make~~ or ~~practice~~ activities).

Teachers often do activities in the class that help students feel excited with their lessons. (Don't say: Teachers often ~~make~~/~~practice~~ activities in the class).

We like to do activities outside. *(Don't say: We like to ~~make~~/~~practice~~ outside).*

We say do homework, (NOT ~~make~~ homework).

She did her homework. *(Don't say: She ~~made~~ her homework).*

He doesn't like to do homework. *(Don't say: He doesn't like to ~~make~~ homework).*

We say do research or carry out research, (NOT ~~make~~ research).

He loves science, so he does research on it and writes about it. *(Don't say: …he ~~makes~~ research on it and writes about it).*

London is one of the best places to carry out a research project. *(Don't say: London is one of the best places to ~~make~~ a research project).*

We say put forward a theory or proposes a theory, (NOT ~~gives~~ a theory).

He wants to propose/put forward a theory of logic. *(Don't say: He wants to ~~give~~ a theory of logic).*

We say tall people, tall trees, tall buildings, (NOT ~~high~~ people, ~~high~~ trees, ~~high~~ buildings).

It is said that tall people need less sleep than short people. *(Don't say: It is said that ~~high~~ people need less sleep than short people).*

Her husband is a tall man. *(Don't say: Her husband is a ~~high~~ man).*

There are many tall trees in the park near my house. *(Don't say: There are many ~~high~~ trees in the park near my house).*

There are a lot of tall buildings in London. *(Don't say: There are a lot of ~~high~~ buildings in London).*

We say high mountain, (NOT ~~tall~~ mountain).

This is a high mountain. *(Don't say: This is a ~~tall~~ mountain).*

He took a big risk when he climbed such high mountain. *(Don't say: He took a big risk when he climbed such ~~tall~~ mountain).*

We say raise your hand, (NOT ~~rise~~ your hand).

Raise your hand if you have any question. *(Don't say: ~~Rise~~ your hand if you have any question).*

If you want to say something, raise your hand. *(Don't say: If you want to say something, ~~rise~~ your hand).*

We say raise taxes, (NOT ~~rises~~ taxes).

They made the decision to raise taxes. *(Don't say: They made the decision to ~~rise~~ taxes).*

We say raise a question, (NOT ~~rise~~ a question).

Do you want to raise a question for me? *(Don't say: Do you want to ~~rise~~ a question for me?).*

We say speak English/Spanish/Japanese, (NOT ~~talk~~ English/Spanish/Japanese).

She can speak English, Spanish, and Japanese. *(Don't say: She can ~~talk~~ English, Spanish, and Japanese).*

Affect is a verb, effect is a noun.

We say affect, (NOT ~~effect~~).

She was affected by cancer. *(Don't say: She was ~~effected~~ by cancer).*

His death affected everyone deeply. *(Don't say: His death ~~effected~~ everyone deeply).*

We say effect, (NOT ~~affect~~).

Her stressful life has had an effect on her health. *(Don't say: Her stressful life has had an ~~affect~~ on her health).*

The medicine had a wonderful effect on her. *(Don't say: The medicine had a wonderful ~~affect~~ on her).*

We say do work, (NOT ~~make~~ work).

We've changed the way we do work at our office. *(Don't say: We've changed the way we ~~make~~ work at our office).*

We do work related to computers. *(Don't say: We ~~make~~ work related to computers).*

We say under a lot of/considerable pressure, (NOT under ~~high~~ pressure).

She's been under a lot of pressure recently. *(Don't say: She's been under ~~high~~ pressure recently).*

He is under considerable pressure to meet deadlines. *(Don't say: He is under ~~high~~ pressure to meet deadlines).*

We say go on strike or stage a strike, (NOT ~~make~~ a strike).

The employees threatened to go on strike. *(Don't say: The employees threatened to ~~make~~ a strike).*

The company profits will decrease if the employees stage a strike. *(Don't say: The company profits will decrease if the employees ~~make~~ a strike).*

We say become aware of the problem, (NOT ~~get aware of~~ the problem).

His family didn't become aware of the problem until the incident took place. *(Don't say: His family didn't ~~get aware of the problem~~ until the incident took place).*

At last, she became aware of her own mistakes. *(Don't say: At last, she ~~got aware of~~ her own mistakes).*

We say a slight decrease/increase, (NOT a ~~little~~ decrease/increase).

There was a slight decrease in the number of unemployed people. *(Don't say: There was a ~~little~~ decrease in the number of unemployed people).*

There has been a slight increase in the number of violent crimes these days. *(Don't say: There has been a ~~little~~ increase in the number of violent crimes these days).*

We say a substantial decrease/increase, (NOT a ~~strong~~ decrease/increase).

There has been a substantial decrease in the number of AIDS cases. *(Don't say: There has been a ~~strong~~ decrease in the number of AIDS cases).*

There has been a substantial increase in the number of homeless people. *(Don't say: There has been a ~~strong~~ increase in the number of homeless people).*

We say X is three times greater than Y, (NOT X is three times ~~larger~~ than Y).

The number of pears is three times greater than the number of apples. *(Don't say: The number of pears is three times ~~larger~~ than the number of apples).*

The number of girls was five times greater than the number of boys. *(Don't say: The number of girls was five times ~~larger~~ than the number of boys).*

We say do the shopping or go shopping, (NOT ~~do shopping~~).

I do the shopping every morning. *(Don't say: I ~~do shopping~~ every morning).*

She intended to go shopping with her mom, but her mom was busy. *(Don't say: She intended to ~~do shopping~~ with her mom, but her mom was busy).*

She has decided to go shopping tomorrow to buy some food. *(Don't say: She has decided to ~~do shopping~~ tomorrow to buy some food).*

We say acquire knowledge, (NOT ~~get~~ knowledge).

Reading helps people acquire knowledge effectively. *(Don't say: Reading helps people ~~get~~ knowledge effectively).*

Experience allows people to acquire knowledge based on the observation. *(Don't say: Experience allows people to ~~get~~ knowledge based on the observation).*

We say do research, (NOT ~~make~~ research).

She spent 4 hours doing research before she started writing. *(Don't say: She spent 4 hours ~~making research~~ before she started writing).*

Students often use the library to do research. *(Don't say: Students often use the library to ~~make research~~).*

We say organise a barbecue or have a barbecue, (NOT ~~make~~ a barbecue).

We organize a barbecue event by the river with our team every weekend. *(Don't say: We make a barbecue event by the river with our team every weekend)*.

They want to have a barbecue to celebrate their decision to buy a new house. *(Don't say: They want to make a barbecue to celebrate their decision to buy a new house)*.

We say come to or arrive at a conclusion, (NOT make a conclusion).

After a long dispute, they finally come to a conclusion. *(Don't say: After a long dispute, they finally make a conclusion)*.

We say someone have a considerable reputation or a well-deserved reputation, (NOT a high reputation).

He has a considerable reputation as a doctor. *(Don't say: He has a high reputation as a doctor)*.

He has a well-deserved reputation as a teacher. *(Don't say: He has a high reputation as a teacher)*.

We say arrive at an agreement or reach an agreement, (NOT get to an agreement or find an agreement).

They arrived at an agreement after three hours' discussion. *(Don't say: They get to an agreement after three hours' discussion)*.

I have reached an agreement with my friend about sharing a car. *(Don't say: I have found an agreement with my friend about sharing a car)*.

We say absolutely vital, (NOT very vital).

It is absolutely vital that you do exactly what I say. *(Don't say: It is very vital that you do exactly what I say)*.

It's absolutely vital that he knows how he is spending his money. *(Don't say: It's very vital that he knows how he is spending his money)*.

We say find a solution, (NOT give a solution).

He is under pressure to find a solution to the problem. *(Don't say: He is under pressure to give a solution to the problem)*.

He is finding a solution to the problem for his boss. *(Don't say: He is giving a solution to the problem for his boss).*

We say make friends, (NOT get friends or find friends).

It's easy to make friends, but hard to get rid of them. *(Don't say: It's easy to get friends, but hard to get rid of them).*

Tom found it difficult to make friends at his new school. *(Don't say: Tom found it difficult to find friends at his new school).*

We say deep dissatisfaction, (NOT strong dissatisfaction).

He expressed his deep dissatisfaction at the way the interview had been conducted. *(Don't say: He expressed his strong dissatisfaction at the way the interview had been conducted).*

We say good/advanced computer skills, (NOT high computer skills).

His good computer skills have been developed through experience. *(Don't say: His high computer skills have been developed through experience).*

Many jobs these days require advanced computer skills. *(Don't say: Many jobs these days require high computer skills).*

We say a good level of education, (NOT a high education).

A good teacher needs to have a good level of education. *(Don't say: A good teacher needs to have a high education).*

To qualify for the job, he must possess a good level of education. *(Don't say: To qualify for the job, he must possess a high education).*

We say a person with good qualifications, (NOT a person with high qualifications).

A teacher with good qualifications is required. *(Don't say: A teacher with high qualifications is required).*

They are professionals with good qualifications and team spirit. *(Don't say: They are professionals with high qualifications and team spirit).*

We say a good/an advanced knowledge of something, (NOT a ~~high~~ knowledge of something).

She has a good knowledge of French. *(Don't say: She has a ~~high~~ knowledge of French).*

The course has enabled students to gain an advanced knowledge of computer programming. *(Don't say: The course has enabled students to gain a ~~high~~ knowledge of computer programming).*

We say an extensive/a comprehensive knowledge of something, (NOT a ~~wide~~ knowledge of something).

He has an extensive knowledge of science. *(Don't say: She has a ~~wide~~ knowledge of French).*

Her brother has a comprehensive knowledge of computing. *(Don't say: Her brother has a ~~wide~~ knowledge of computing).*

We say a person has considerable experience of something, (NOT a person has ~~big/great/wide~~ experience of something).

The lawyer has considerable experience of criminal law. *(Don't say: The lawyer has ~~great~~ experience of criminal law).*

She has considerable experience of teaching. *(Don't say: She has ~~wide~~ experience of teaching).*

We say establish/develop a good relationship with someone, (NOT ~~get~~ a good relationship with someone).

The new worker finds it hard to establish a good relationship with his employer. *(Don't say: The new worker finds it hard to ~~get~~ a good relationship with his employer).*

He has developed a good relationship with all workers he's worked with. *(Don't say: He ~~has got~~ a good relationship with all workers he's worked with).*

We say make mistakes, (NOT ~~do~~ mistakes).

Students tend to make mistakes with the passive voice. *(Don't say: Students tend to ~~do~~ mistakes with the passive voice).*

She tends to make a lot of mistakes while typing. *(Don't say: She tends to ~~do~~ a lot of mistakes while typing).*

We say have problems or experience problems, (NOT ~~get~~ problems).

He had problems with his lungs. *(Don't say: He ~~got problems~~ with his lungs).*

Customers have experienced problems in finding parking places at the supermarket. *(Don't say: Customers ~~have got~~ problems in finding parking places at the supermarket).*

We say problems arise or occur, (NOT problems ~~happen~~).

The problems arise due to an error in our calculations. *(Don't say: The problems ~~happen~~ due to an error in our calculations).*

The indigestion problems occur due to various stimulants, such as spicy foods or alcohol. *(Don't say: The indigestion problems ~~happen~~ due to various stimulants, such as spicy foods or alcohol).*

We say difficulties arise, (NOT difficulties ~~appear~~).

Difficulties arise due to a language barrier. *(Don't say: Difficulties ~~appear~~ due to a language barrier).*

We say small minority, amount, number, quantity, percentage, (NOT ~~little~~ minority, amount, number, quantity, percentage).

Only a small minority of students are interested in politics these days. *(Don't say: Only a ~~little~~ minority of students are interested in politics these days).*

Only a small amount of water is used. *(Don't say: Only a ~~little~~ amount of water is used).*

Only a small number of automobiles were produced this year. *(Don't say: Only a ~~little number of~~ automobiles were produced this year).*

There is a small quantity of milk in the jug. *(Don't say: There is ~~a little quantity of~~ milk in the jug).*

Only a small percentage of people are interested in the arts. *(Don't say: Only a little percentage of people are interested in the arts).*

We say large quantity, amount, number, majority, percentage, (NOT great/big/high quantity, amount, number, majority, percentage).

The police seized a large quantity of drugs at the bar. *(Don't say: The police seized a great/big/high quantity of drugs at the bar).*

Tom borrowed a large amount of money from his girlfriend. *(Don't say: Tom borrowed a great/big/high amount of money from his girlfriend).*

A large number of invitations have been sent. *(Don't say: A great/big/high number of invitations have been sent).*

A large majority of South Africans are black and poor. *(Don't say: A great/big/high majority of South Africans are black and poor).*

A large percentage of the students do not speak English at home. *(Don't say: A great/big/high percentage of the students do not speak English at home).*

We say increase dramatically or significantly, (NOT increase strongly).

The cost of living has increased dramatically. *(Don't say: The cost of living has increased strongly).*

Our profits have increased significantly over the past three years. *(Don't say: Our profits have increased strongly over the past three years).*

We say make an effort, (NOT do an effort).

You must make an effort to stop smoking. *(Don't say: You must do an effort to stop smoking).*

He makes an effort to be a better person. *(Don't say: He does an effort to be a better person).*

We say absolutely delighted, (NOT very delighted).

Her parents were absolutely delighted about the baby. *(Don't say: Her parents very delighted about the baby).*

She gave him a birthday present and he was absolutely delighted. *(Don't say: She gave him a birthday present and he was ~~very~~ delighted).*

We say a great pleasure, (NOT a ~~big~~ pleasure).

It's a great pleasure for me to be here. *(Don't say: It's a ~~big~~ pleasure for me to be here).*

It is a great pleasure being with you. *(Don't say: It's a ~~big~~ pleasure being with you).*

We say absolutely furious, (NOT ~~very~~ furious).

He looks absolutely furious. *(Don't say: He looks ~~very~~ furious).*

My father was not just annoyed, he was absolutely furious. *(Don't say: My father was not just annoyed, he was ~~very~~ furious).*

We say five hundred thousand = 500,000 (NOT five hundred thousand~~s~~).

I'd like to borrow about five hundred thousand dollars. *(Don't say: I'd like to borrow about five hundred thousand~~s~~ dollars).*

We say two million dollars = $2,000,000 (NOT two million~~s~~ ~~dollar~~).

The kidnapper demanded a ransom of two million dollars. *(Don't say: The kidnapper demanded a ransom of two million~~s~~ ~~dollar~~).*

There are three hundred thousand volunteers, and almost four million school children. *(Don't say: There are three hundred thousand volunteers, and almost four million~~s~~ school children).*

We say enjoy playing computer games (NOT enjoy ~~to play~~ computer games).

He really enjoys playing computer games. *(Don't say: He really enjoys ~~to play~~ computer games).*

She really enjoys reading comic books. *(Don't say: She really enjoys ~~to read~~ comic books).*

We say look forward to visiting, (NOT look forward ~~to visit~~ your reply).

We look forward to visiting you next week. *(Don't say: We look forward to visit you next week)*.

I am looking forward to hearing from you soon. *(Don't say: I am looking forward to hear from you soon)*.

We say feel + adjective + v-ing, (NOT feel + adjective + to-inf).

Tom didn't feel comfortable driving his friend's new car. *(Don't say: Tom didn't feel comfortable to drive his friend's new car)*.

We feel happy watching this movie. *(Don't say: We feel happy to watch this movie)*.

We say be + adjective + to-inf, (NOT be + adjective + v-ing).

I was happy to see him when he arrived. *(Don't say: I was happy seeing him)*.

We say be + adjective + enough + to-inf, (NOT be + adjective + enough + v-ing).

This video was easy enough to understand. *(Don't say: This video was easy enough understanding)*.

We say allow + object + to-inf, (NOT allow + object + v-ing).

Her parents won't allow her to stay out late. *(Don't say: Her parents won't allow her staying out late)*.

His father didn't allow him to smoke cigarettes. *(Don't say: His father didn't allow him to smoking cigarettes)*.

We say be allowed + to-inf, (NOT be allowed + v-ing).

We were not allowed to talk about sex in the class. *(Don't say: We were not allowed talking about sex in the class)*.

She was not allowed to go out on weekday nights. *(Don't say: She was not allowed going out on weekday nights)*.

We say make + object + bare infinitive, (NOT make + object + to-inf).

He made her feel sad. *(Don't say: He made her ~~to feel~~ sad).*

You made me feel happy. *(Don't say: You made me ~~to feel~~ happy).*

We say be advised, be allowed, be forbidden, be made, be permitted + To-inf, (NOT be advised, be allowed, be forbidden, be made, be permitted + ~~V-ing~~).

He was advised to be punctual. *(Don't say: He was advised to ~~being~~ punctual).*

As a child, he was allowed to go to bed when he wanted. *(Don't say: As a child, he was allowed ~~going~~ to bed when he wanted).*

She was forbidden to marry the man next door. *(Don't say: She was forbidden ~~marrying~~ the man next door).*

I was made to wait more than an hour. *(Don't say: I was made ~~waiting~~ more than an hour).*

He was permitted to bring his camera into the concert. *(Don't say: He was permitted ~~bringing~~ his camera into the concert).*

We say suggest + v-ing, (NOT suggest + ~~to-inf~~).

He suggested going for a walk. *(Don't say: He suggested ~~to go~~ for a walk).*

I suggested going for a drink. *(Don't say: I suggested ~~to go~~ for a drink).*

John suggested going to a movie. (Don't say: John ~~suggested to go~~ to a movie).

Except (verb): means to not include something/somebody.

Accept (verb): means to receive willingly something that is offered.

We say accept a gift, (NOT ~~except~~ a gift).

Please accept my gift. *(Don't say: Please ~~except~~ my gift).*

Advise is a verb.

Advice is a noun.

We say take someone's advice, (NOT take someone's ~~advise~~).

We do not always take his advice. (Don't say: we do not always take his ~~advise~~).

We say cannot, (NOT ~~can not~~).

I cannot go shopping without my credit card. *(Don't say: I ~~can not~~ go shopping...).*

I cannot go anywhere tonight. *(Don't say: I ~~can not~~ go anywhere tonight).*

Affect is a verb.

Effect is a noun.

Using a computer all day has really affected his eyesight. *(Don't say: Using a computer all day has really ~~effected~~ his eyesight).*

The cold weather has really affected my health. *(Don't say: The cold weather has really ~~effected~~ my health).*

Everyday is an adjective that means "daily"

Every day is an adverb of frequency.

I use my mobile phone every day. *(Don't say: I use my mobile phone ~~everyday~~).*

He drinks a lot of water every day. *(Don't say: He drinks a lot of water ~~everyday~~).*

This is an outfit for everyday use. *(Don't say: This is an outfit for ~~every day~~ use).*

These shoes are great for everyday wear. *(Don't say: These shoes are great for ~~every day~~ wear).*

We say forty, (NOT ~~fourty~~).

Forty people attended the party. *(Don't say: ~~Fourty~~ people attended the party).*

I spent forty dollars and had twenty left. *(Don't say: I spent ~~fourty~~ dollars and had twenty left).*

We say don't get any water, (NOT don't get ~~no~~ water).

We don't get any water. *(Don't say: We don't get no water).*

He didn't get any help. *(Don't say: He didn't get no help).*

We say uninterested in something, (NOT disinterested in something).

He was uninterested in this book. *(Don't say: He was disinterested in this book).*

She becomes uninterested in her job. *(Don't say: She becomes disinterested in her job).*

We say either…is, (NOT either…are).

Either he or she is going to the party. *(Don't say: Either he or she are going to the party).*

Either he or she is going to attend the meeting. *(Don't say: Either he or she are going to attend the meeting).*

Either he or she is cleaning the windows. *(Don't say: Either he or she are cleaning the windows).*

Either he or she cooks dinner. *(Don't say: Either he or she cook dinner).*

We say on the water, (NOT in the water).

There was a boat floating on the water. *(Don't say: There was a boat floating in the water).*

A leaf is floating on the water. *(Don't say: A leaf is floating in the water).*

We use less (NOT fewer) with uncountable nouns.

He has less money than she does. *(Don't say: He has fewer money than she does).*

You should eat less fast food. *(Don't say: You should eat fewer fast food).*

We use fewer (NOT less) with countable nouns.

Tom has fewer friends than his brother. *(Don't say: Tom has less friends than his brother).*

Mary has fewer books than her brother. *(Don't say: Mary has less books than her brother).*

We say accuse somebody of something, (NOT accuse somebody ~~for~~ something).

She accused him of stealing her car. *(Don't say: She accused him ~~for~~ stealing her car).*

The police accused him of murder. *(Don't say: The police accused him ~~for~~ murder).*

We say accustomed to, (NOT accustomed ~~with~~).

She will soon become accustomed to the noise of the city. *(Don't say: She will soon become accustomed ~~with~~ the noise of the city).*

He became accustomed to the food in Italy. *(Don't say: He became accustomed ~~with~~ the food in Italy).*

We say anxious about, (NOT anxious ~~for~~).

She is anxious about her father's health. *(Don't say: She is anxious ~~for~~ her father's health).*

Tom is anxious about his upcoming surgery. *(Don't say: Tom is anxious ~~for~~ his upcoming surgery).*

He is a little anxious about his job right now. *(Don't say: He is a little anxious ~~for~~ his job right now).*

We say ashamed of, (NOT ashamed ~~about~~).

Tom feels ashamed of the lies he told. *(Don't say: Tom feels ashamed ~~about~~ the lies he told).*

She was deeply ashamed of her behavior. *(Don't say: She was deeply ashamed ~~about~~ her behavior).*

He felt so ashamed of himself for making such a fuss. *(Don't say: He felt so ashamed ~~about~~ himself for making such a fuss).*

We say believe in, (NOT believe ~~at~~).

She believes in the power of love. *(Don't say: She believes at the power of love).*

We believe in gods. *(Don't say: We believe at gods).*

He believed in himself. *(Don't say: He believed at himself).*

We say boast of or about, (NOT boast for).

She boasted of having won the prize. *(Don't say: She boasted for having won the prize).*

Tom boasted about his accomplishments. *(Don't say: Tom boasted for his accomplishments).*

We say complain about, (NOT complain for).

Mary complained about the noise. *(Don't say: Mary complained for the noise).*

Tom complained about his low salary. *(Don't say: Tom complained for his low salary).*

We say composed of, (NOT composed with).

This cloth is composed of wool and silk. *(Don't say: This cloth is composed with wool and silk).*

The pie is composed of seven pieces. *(Don't say: The pie is composed with seven pieces).*

We say confidence in, (NOT confidence about).

I have confidence in him. *(Don't say: I have confidence about him).*

Mary has confidence in Tom's ability to win the race. *(Don't say: Mary has confidence about Tom's ability to win the race).*

We say die of/from an illness, (NOT die about an illness).

He died of cancer. *(Don't say: He died about cancer).*

She died from a heart attack. *(Don't say: She died about a heart attack).*

We say different from, (NOT different with).

Her car is different from mine. *(Don't say: Her car is different ~~with~~ mine).*

My book is different from yours. *(Don't say: My book is different ~~with~~ yours).*

We say divide into, (NOT divide ~~to~~).

The exam was divided into two parts. *(Don't say: The exam was divided ~~to~~ two parts).*

She divided the cake into six pieces. *(Don't say: She divided the cake ~~to~~ six pieces).*

We say no doubt about, (NOT no doubt ~~in~~ or ~~for~~).

There's no doubt about her ability. *(Don't say: There's no doubt ~~in~~ her ability).*

There was no doubt about the answer. *(Don't say: There was no doubt ~~for~~ the answer).*

There was no doubt about the problem they had to solve. *(Don't say: There was no doubt ~~in/for~~ the problem they had to solve).*

We say dressed in blue, (NOT dressed ~~with~~ blue).

Tom was dressed in blue. *(Don't say: Tom was dressed ~~with~~ blue).*

The bridesmaids were dressed in pink. *(Don't say: The bridesmaids were dressed ~~with~~ pink).*

We say exchange for, (NOT exchange ~~with~~).

He exchanged his currency for dollars in the hotel. *(Don't say: He exchanged his currency ~~with~~ dollars in the hotel).*

I exchanged the T-shirt for a larger size. *(Don't say: I exchanged the T-shirt ~~with~~ a larger size).*

We say fail in, (NOT fail ~~from/with~~).

Tom failed in his attempt to swim across the river. *(Don't say: Tom failed ~~with~~ his attempt to swim across the river).*

She failed in her attempt to persuade him. *(Don't say: She failed ~~from~~ her attempt to persuade him).*

We say be full of, (NOT full ~~with~~).

He is full of hope. *(Don't say: He is full ~~with~~ hope).*

He is full of energy. *(Don't say: He is full ~~with~~ energy).*

Nature is full of mystery. *(Don't say: Nature is full ~~with~~ mystery).*

We say guilty of, (NOT guilty ~~for~~).

He was guilty of murder. *(Don't say: He was guilty ~~for~~ murder).*

The man was guilty of robbery. *(Don't say: The man was guilty ~~for~~ robbery).*

We say insist on, (NOT insist ~~in~~).

He insisted on staying with her for a while. *(Don't say: He insisted ~~in~~ staying with her for a while).*

She insisted on doing everything herself. *(Don't say: She insisted ~~in~~ doing everything herself).*

We say be jealous of, (NOT jealous ~~about~~).

Mary has always been jealous of Susan's long blonde hair. *(Don't say: Mary has always been jealous ~~about~~ Susan's long blonde hair).*

Tom was jealous of his brother's wealth. *(Don't say: Tom was jealous ~~about~~ his brother's wealth).*

We say leave for a place, (NOT ~~leave~~ to a place).

We are leaving for London tomorrow night. *(Don't say: We are leaving ~~to~~ London tomorrow night).*

She is leaving for Canada tomorrow. *(Don't say: She is leaving ~~to~~ Canada tomorrow).*

We say look at, (NOT look ~~to~~).

She didn't look at him and he didn't look at her. *(Don't say: She didn't look ~~to~~ him and he didn't look ~~to~~ her).*

Look at the beautiful house over there. *(Don't say: Look to the beautiful house over there).*

We say married to, (NOT married with).

Tom's getting married to Mary in June. *(Don't say: Tom's getting married with Mary in June).*

She is married to my cousin. *(Don't say: She is married with my cousin).*

We say opposite to, (NOT opposite from).

He lives in the house opposite to ours. *(Don't say: He lives in the house opposite from ours).*

She lives in the house opposite to mine. *(Don't say: She lives in the house opposite from mine).*

We say be related to, (NOT related with).

He is related to her by marriage. *(Don't say: He is related with her by marriage).*

Are you related to him? *(Don't say: Are you related with him?).*

No, I'm not related to him. *(Don't say: No, I'm not related with him).*

We say be similar to, (NOT be similar with).

Your problem is similar to mine. *(Don't say: Your problem is similar with mine).*

You two look very similar to each other. *(Don't say: You two look very similar with each other).*

We say sit at a desk, (NOT sit on a desk).

He doesn't want to sit at a desk all day. *(Don't say: He doesn't want to sit on a desk all day).*

She knows sitting at a desk all day is really bad for her. *(Don't say: She knows sitting on a desk all day is really bad for her).*

We say spend on, (NOT spend for).

He spends a lot of time on playing computer games every day. *(Don't say: He spends a lot of time for playing computer games every day).*

Tom spends hours on the phone talking to his girlfriend. *(Don't say: Tom spends hours on the phone for talking to his girlfriend).*

We say succeed in, (NOT succeed at).

He wants to succeed in running a business. *(Don't say: He wants to succeed at running a business).*

Not everybody succeeds in this business. *(Don't say: Not everybody succeeds at this business).*

We say superior to, (NOT superior from or than).

I think city life is superior to country life in many respects. *(Don't say: I think city life is superior from country life in many respects).*

This material is superior to that. *(Don't say: This material is superior than that).*

He is superior to me in strength. *(Don't say: He is superior than me in strength).*

We say be sure of, (NOT be sure for).

He was sure of his decision. *(Don't say: He was sure for his decision).*

Tom was never very sure of himself as a comedian. *(Don't say: Tom was never very sure for himself as a comedian).*

I just think she was never very sure of herself as a parent. *(Don't say: I just think she was never very sure for herself as a parent).*

We say suspect somebody/something of doing something, (NOT suspect somebody/something for doing something).

We suspect him of telling a lie. *(Don't say: We suspect him for telling a lie).*

The police suspect him of being the murder. *(Don't say: The police suspect him for being the murder).*

We say be tired of, (NOT be tired with).

He is sick and tired of eating hamburgers. *(Don't say: He is sick and tired of eating hamburgers).*

I'm really tired of your complaints. *(Don't say: I'm really tired ~~with~~ your complaints).*

I'm tired of listening to her boasts. *(Don't say: I'm tired ~~with~~ listening to her boasts).*

We say translate into, (NOT translate ~~to~~).

Could you translate this sentence into English? *(Don't say: Could you translate this sentence ~~to~~ English?).*

Please translate this message into Chinese. *(Don't say: Please translate this message ~~to~~ Chinese).*

We say be capable of doing something, (NOT be capable ~~to do~~ something).

She is capable of teaching Japanese. *(Don't say: She is capable ~~to teach~~ Japanese).*

Tom is capable of keeping a secret when he wants to. *(Don't say: Tom is capable ~~to keep~~ a secret when he wants to).*

We say object to + V-ing, (NOT object to + ~~bare infinitive~~).

He objected to being treated like a child. *(Don't say: He objected ~~to be~~ treated like a child).*

She objected to being called greedy. *(Don't say: She objected ~~to be~~ called greedy).*

We say would you mind + V-ing, (NOT would you mind + ~~To-inf~~).

Would you mind opening the window? *(Don't say: Would you mind ~~to open~~ the window?).*

Would you mind watching my laptop for a few minutes? *(Don't say: Would you mind ~~to watch~~ my laptop for a few minutes?).*

We say have difficulty in doing something, (NOT have difficulty ~~to do~~ something).

He still has difficulty in making himself understood in Japanese. *(Don't say: He still has difficulty ~~to make~~ himself understood in Japanese).*

I have difficulty in learning Chinese. *(Don't say: I have difficulty ~~to learn~~ Chinese).*

We say it's no use doing something, (NOT it's no use ~~to do~~ something).

It's no use asking him for advice. *(Don't say: It's no use ~~to ask~~ him for advice).*

It's no use trying to convince her. *(Don't say: It's no use ~~to try~~ to convince her).*

We say it's no good doing something, (NOT it's no good ~~to do~~ something).

It's no good trying to persuade him to come with us. *(Don't say: It's no good ~~to try~~ to persuade him to come with us).*

It's no good talking to this man. *(Don't say: It's no good ~~to talk~~ to this man).*

We say look forward to doing something, (NOT look forward to ~~do~~ something).

I look forward to visiting my grandparents next week. *(Don't say: I look forward ~~to visit~~ my grandparents next week).*

I am looking forward to hearing from you soon. *(Don't say: I am looking forward ~~to hear~~ from you soon).*

I look forward to talking with you. *(Don't say: I look forward ~~to talk~~ with you).*

We say the door of the car, (NOT ~~the car's door~~).

The man unlocked the door of the car. *(Don't say: The man unlocked ~~the car's door~~).*

He opened the door of the car. *(Don't say: He opened ~~the car's door~~).*

We say it was she, (NOT it was ~~her~~).

It was she who somehow knew you best. *(Don't say: It was ~~her~~ who somehow knew you best).*

It was he who decided we should go to Moscow. *(Don't say: It was ~~him~~ who decided we should go to Moscow).*

We say he is taller than I (am), (NOT he is taller than ~~me~~).

He is taller than I (am). *(Don't say: He is taller than ~~me~~).*

Jane's sister is more beautiful than she is. *(Don't say: Jane's sister is more beautiful than ~~her~~).*

We say between you and me, (NOT between you and ~~I~~).

Let's keep this as a secret between you and me. *(Don't say: Let's keep this as a secret between you and ~~I~~).*

I hope you can keep this as a secret between you and me. *(Don't say: I hope you can keep this as a secret between you and ~~I~~).*

The difference between you and me is that I am aware of this matter. *(Don't say: The difference between you and ~~I~~ is that I am aware of this matter).*

We say a friend of mine (NOT a friend of ~~me~~ or ~~my~~).

Peter is a friend of mine. *(Don't say: Peter is a friend of ~~me~~).*

Thank you for being a friend of mine. *(Don't say: Thank you for being a friend of ~~my~~).*

We say themselves, (NOT ~~theirselves~~).

Parents usually blame themselves for the way their kids behave. *(Don't say: Parents usually blame ~~theirselves~~ for the way their kids behave).*

They hurt themselves in the car accident. *(Don't say: They hurt ~~theirselves~~ in the car accident).*

We say the same as, (NOT the same ~~with~~).

His car is the same as mine. *(Don't say: His car is the same ~~with~~ mine).*

His taste in music is almost the same as mine. *(Don't say: His taste in music is almost the same ~~with~~ mine).*

We say like something very much, (NOT ~~very~~ like something).

I like the film very much. *(Don't say: I ~~very~~ like the film).*

He likes the food my mother cooks very much. *(Don't say: He ~~very~~ likes the food my mother cooks).*

We say neither ... nor, (NOT neither...~~or~~).

Neither my brother nor my sister went to university. *(Don't say: Neither my brother ~~or~~ my sister went to university).*

I can speak neither Japanese nor French. *(Don't say: I can speak neither Japanese ~~or~~ French).*

We say either ... or, (NOT either...~~nor~~).

She can speak either French or English. *(Don't say: She can speak either French ~~nor~~ English).*

She wants to play either guitar or piano. *(Don't say: She wants to play either guitar ~~nor~~ piano).*

We use neither in a negative sentence, (NOT ~~both~~).

Neither of them were involved in the traffic accident. *(Don't say: ~~both of them~~ were involved in the traffic accident).*

Neither of us were in London at that time. *(Don't say: ~~both of us~~ were in London at that time).*

We use either in a negative sentence, (NOT ~~too~~ or ~~also~~).

If you don't come, he won't come either. *(Don't say: If you don't come, he won't come ~~too/also~~).*

I don't want to eat hamburger either. *(Don't say: I don't want to eat hamburger ~~too/also~~).*

We say give a discount, (NOT ~~make~~ a discount).

Could you give me a discount? *(Don't say: Could you give ~~make~~ a discount?).*

The shopkeeper gave me a discount of 10%. *(Don't say: The shopkeeper ~~made~~ me a discount of 10%).*

We say give or deliver a lecture, (NOT make a lecture).

The professor gave a lecture on finance. *(Don't say: The professor made a lecture on finance).*

The teacher delivered a lecture about the importance of education. *(Don't say: The teacher made a lecture about the importance of education).*

We say make a mistake, (NOT do a mistake).

Sometimes he makes a mistake and does the wrong thing. *(Don't say: Sometimes he does a mistake and does the wrong thing).*

He admitted that he had made a mistake. *(Don't say: He admitted that he had done a mistake).*

We say tell or speak the truth, (NOT say the truth).

To tell the truth, I do not remember meeting him. *(Don't say: To say the truth, I do not remember meeting him).*

To tell the truth, she is still under thirty. *(Don't say: To say the truth, she is still under thirty).*

To tell the truth, I don't like her. *(Don't say: To say the truth, I don't like her).*

We say listen to someone or something, (NOT listen someone or something).

I was listening to music. *(Don't say: I was listening music).*

She loves listening to the sound of falling rain. *(Don't say: She loves listening the sound of falling rain).*

We say pay for something, (NOT pay something).

I'll pay for your ticket. *(Don't say: I'll pay your ticket).*

Let me pay for dinner this time. *(Don't say: Let me pay dinner this time).*

We say remind somebody about/of something, (NOT remind somebody for something).

He reminded me of my promise. *(Don't say: He reminded me for my promise)*.

He reminded me of the meeting tomorrow. *(Don't say: He reminded me for the meeting tomorrow)*.

We say reply to someone, (NOT reply someone).

He replied to my email yesterday. *(Don't say: He replied my email yesterday)*.

She hasn't replied to my letter yet. *(Don't say: She hasn't replied my letter yet)*.

We say say to someone, (NOT say someone).

He said to me that he would come at 7 pm. *(Don't say: He said me that he would come at 7 pm)*.

She said to me that I ought to wait for her. *(Don't say: She said me that I ought to wait for her)*.

We say wait for someone or something, (NOT wait someone or something).

I will be waiting for you at the mall. *(Don't say: I will be waiting you at the mall)*.

I'm waiting for a response from him. *(Don't say: I'm waiting a response from him)*.

We say write to someone, (NOT write someone).

I hope you will write to your mother when you have time. *(Don't say: I hope you will write your mother when you have time)*.

He is very happy to write to her every week. *(Don't say: He is very happy to write her every week)*.

We say she/he plays guitar very well, (NOT she/he play guitar very well).

She speaks English fluently. *(Don't say: She speak English fluently)*.

He runs very fast. *(Don't say: He run very fast)*.

We say he knows how to play the piano, (NOT he knows to play the piano).

I know how to defend myself. *(Don't say: I ~~know to~~ defend myself).*

She knows how to speak French. *(Don't say: She ~~knows to~~ speak French).*

We say he is taller than everybody else, (NOT ~~he is taller than everybody~~).

He runs faster than everybody else. *(Don't say: He runs faster than everybody).*

She is smarter than everybody else in her class. *(Don't say: She is smarter than everybody in her class).*

We say I asked my mom for some money, but she had none, (NOT I asked my mom for some money, but she ~~had not~~).

My daughter asked me for some candies, but I had none. *(Don't say: My daughter asked me for some candies, but I had ~~not~~).*

The boy asked his mother for some cakes, but she had none. *(Don't say: The boy asked his mother for some cakes, but she had ~~not~~).*

We say answer someone's question, (NOT answer ~~to~~ someone's question).

She didn't know how to answer her teacher's question. *(Don't say: She didn't know how to ~~answer to~~ her teacher's question).*

She failed to answer my question. *(Don't say: She failed to ~~answer to~~ my question).*

We say approach a place, (NOT approach ~~to~~ a place).

Don't approach that house. *(Don't say: Don't approach ~~to~~ that house).*

Don't let anyone approach this room. *(Don't say: Don't let anyone approach ~~to~~ this room).*

The cat slowly approached the bush where the mouse was hiding. *(Don't say: The cat slowly approached ~~to~~ the bush where the mouse was hiding).*

We say enter the room, (NOT enter ~~into~~ the room).

I saw her enter the room. *(Don't say: I saw her enter ~~into~~ the room).*

My mother saw a stranger enter that house. *(Don't say: My mother saw a stranger enter ~~into~~ that house).*

We say obey someone, (NOT obey ~~to~~ someone).

I always obey my parents. *(Don't say: I always obey ~~to~~ my parents).*

Tom doesn't always obey his father. *(Don't say: Tom doesn't always obey ~~to~~ his father).*

We say let someone do something, (NOT let someone ~~to do~~ something).

Let him stay in the room. *(Don't say: Let him ~~to~~ stay in the room).*

Don't let him leave the house. *(Don't say: Don't let him ~~to~~ leave the house).*

We say tell someone, (NOT ~~tell to~~ someone).

You should tell him the truth. *(Don't say: You should tell ~~to~~ him the truth).*

If Mary phones, tell her to meet me at the cinema. *(Don't say: If Mary phones, tell ~~to~~ her to meet me at the cinema).*

She told me that she was tired. *(Don't say: She ~~told to~~ me that she was tired).*

His boss told him to be on time. *(Don't say: His boss ~~told to~~ him to be on time).*

We say make someone do something, (NOT make someone ~~to do~~ something).

I couldn't make her understand my Japanese. *(Don't say: I couldn't make her ~~to~~ understand my Japanese).*

Can you make her laugh and feel attracted to you? *(Don't say: Can you make her ~~to~~ laugh and feel attracted to you?).*

We say watch somebody do/doing something, (NOT watch somebody ~~to do~~ something).

We sat and watched the kids playing in the water. *(Don't say: We sat and watched the kids ~~to play~~ in the water).*

We watched the professor speak to a crowd of students yesterday. *(Don't say: We watched the professor ~~to speak~~ to a crowd of students yesterday).*

We say hear somebody do/doing something, (NOT hear somebody ~~to do~~

something).

I heard her talking about you by the pool yesterday. *(Don't say: I heard her to talk about you by the pool yesterday).*

I heard you talk on the phone as I walked past your office. *(Don't say: I heard you to talk on the phone as I walked past your office).*

We say feel somebody do/doing something, (NOT feel somebody to do something).

She felt a hand touching her shoulder. *(Don't say: She felt a hand to touch her shoulder).*

He felt something crawl up his arm. *(Don't say: He felt something to crawl up his arm).*

We say he went to the mall and bought clothes, (NOT he went to the mall and he bought clothes).

We went to the restaurant and enjoyed seafood. *(Don't say: We went to the restaurant and we enjoyed seafood).*

He went to the library and read book. *(Don't say: He went to the library and he read book).*

We say return to, (NOT return back to).

Tom returned to work yesterday. *(Don't say: Tom returned back to work yesterday).*

She returned to Paris from London yesterday. *(Don't say: She returned back to Paris from London yesterday).*

We say be + adjective + enough, (NOT be + enough + adjective).

This T-shirt is big enough to fit me. *(Don't say: This T-shirt is enough big to fit me).*

This novel is interesting enough to read. *(Don't say: This novel is enough interesting to read).*

We say till/until next month, (NOT ~~to~~ next month).

Can you wait until next month? *(Don't say: Can you wait ~~to~~ next month?).*

The meeting will be postponed until next week. *(Don't say: The meeting will be postponed ~~to~~ next week).*

His father used to drink till late at night. *(Don't say: His father used to drink ~~to~~ late at night).*

I won't be able to see him till next week. *(Don't say: I won't be able to see him ~~to~~ next week).*

We say come into, (NOT ~~come in~~).

He came into the office today. *(Don't say: He ~~came in~~ the office today).*

She came into the kitchen. *(Don't say: She ~~came in~~ the kitchen).*

We say in the afternoon, (NOT ~~at~~ the afternoon).

I am going to play football in the afternoon. *(Don't say: I am going to play football ~~at~~ the afternoon).*

I have English class in the afternoon. *(Don't say: I have English class ~~at~~ the afternoon).*

We say with a knife, (NOT ~~by~~ a knife).

She cut the meat with a knife. *(Don't say: She cut the meat ~~by~~ a knife).*

She killed him with a gun. *(Don't say: She killed him ~~by~~ a knife).*

We say lie down, (NOT ~~lay down~~).

I need to lie down for an hour. *(Don't say: I need to ~~lay down~~ for an hour).*

She told me she was going to lie down on the sofa. *(Don't say: She told me she was going to ~~lay down~~ on the sofa).*

To borrow means *to get something from someone.*

To lend means *to give something to someone.*

We say borrow, (NOT ~~lend~~).

I want to borrow some money from you. *(Don't say: I want to ~~lend~~ some money from you).*

He doesn't want to borrow money from the bank to buy a house. *(Don't say: He doesn't want to ~~lend~~ money from the bank to buy a house).*

We say lend, (NOT ~~borrow~~).

Could you lend me your car tonight? *(Don't say: Could you ~~borrow~~ me your car tonight?).*

Could you lend me a few dollars for dinner, please? *(Don't say: Could you ~~borrow~~ me a few dollars for dinner, please?).*

To refuse means *not to take what someone has offered to you or not to do what someone asks you to do.*

To deny means *to say that something isn't true or to refuse to admit or accept something.*

We say refuse, (NOT ~~deny~~).

Mary refused to go out with Tom. *(Don't say: Mary ~~deny~~ to go out with Tom).*

She refused to answer any questions concerning her private life. *(Don't say: She ~~deny~~ to answer any questions concerning her private life).*

We say deny, (NOT ~~refuse~~).

He denied that he had stolen anything. *(Don't say: He ~~refused~~ that he had stolen anything).*

Mary denied that she had seen Tom. *(Don't say: Mary ~~refused~~ that she had seen Tom).*

We say late, (NOT ~~lately~~).

Yesterday I went to work late. *(Don't say: Yesterday I went to work ~~lately~~).*

This morning, he went to school late. *(Don't say: This morning, he went to school lately)*.

Few means *not many.*

A few means *some, or a small number of something.*

We say few, (NOT a few).

Few people live to be 100 years old. *(Don't say: a few people live to be 100 years old)*.

Few students like exams. *(Don't say: a few students like exams)*.

We say a few, (NOT few).

There are a few students in the class. *(Don't say: There are few students in the class)*.

Only a few people speak Japanese as a mother language. *(Don't say: Only few people speak Japanese as a mother language)*.

Little means *not much.*

A little means *a small amount of something.*

We say little, (NOT a little).

I have little money. *(Don't say: I have a little money)*.

There is little water in the bucket. *(Don't say: There is a little water in the bucket)*.

We say a little, (NOT little).

There is a little milk in the glass. *(Don't say: There is little milk in the glass)*.

He added a little sugar to his tea. *(Don't say: He added little sugar to his tea)*.

We say older than, (NOT elder than).

John is older than Peter. *(Don't say: John is elder than Peter)*.

She is older than I am. *(Don't say: She is elder than I am)*.

Adj ending with V-ing is used to describe *a thing that causes the emotion - how a person affects to people.*

Adj ending with V-ed is used to describe emotions - *how people feels about something.*

We say an interesting film, (NOT an ~~interested~~ film).

I have watched an interesting film. *(Don't say: I have watched an ~~interested~~ film).*

She gave me an interesting book yesterday. *(Don't say: She gave me an ~~interested~~ book yesterday).*

We say feel bored, (NOT ~~feel boring~~).

Do you feel bored when you go out with him? *(Don't say: Do you ~~feel boring~~ when you go out with him?).*

I feel excited to see you. *(Don't say: I ~~feel exciting~~ to see you).*

I think this film is boring, so I feel bored. *(Don't say: I think this film is boring, so I ~~feel boring~~).*

Less is used with uncountable nouns.

Fewer is used with plural nouns.

We say less money, (NOT ~~fewer money~~).

I have less money than he has. *(Don't say: I have ~~fewer money~~ than he has).*

I have less time than we thought I had. *(Don't say: I have ~~fewer time~~ than we thought I had).*

We say fewer people, (NOT ~~less people~~).

I have fewer apples than you. *(Don't say: I have ~~less apples~~ than you).*

There were fewer people than we had expected at the party. *(Don't say: There were ~~less people~~ than we had expected at the party).*

Customer mean *a person who buys something from a shop or store.*

Client means *a person who uses the services or advice of a professional person such as a doctor or lawyer.*

We say customer, (NOT client).

That shop has many customers. *(Don't say: That shop has many clients).*

We had a lot of customers yesterday. *(Don't say: We had a lot of clients yesterday).*

We say client, (NOT customer).

He is a famous lawyer who has many famous clients. *(Don't say: He is a famous lawyer who has many famous customers).*

I am his client. *(Don't say: I am his customer).*

We say much/far younger than, (NOT very younger than).

He's much/far younger than I am. *(Don't say: He's very younger than I am.)*

Her husband is much/far older than she is. *(Don't say: Her husband is very older than she is).*

Chinese is much/far more difficult than French. *(Don't say: Chinese is very more difficult than French).*

We say a journey, (NOT a travel). Travel is uncountable.

We had a long journey through the mountains. *(Don't say: We had a long travel through the mountains).*

We had a long journey by coach from the north to the south of the country. *(Don't say: We had a long travel by coach from the north to the south of the country).*

I wish you a good journey! *(Don't say: I wish you a good travel!).*

We say a loaf of bread, (NOT a bread). Bread is uncountable.

She bought a loaf of bread. *(Don't say: She bought a bread).*

She taught me how to make a loaf of bread. *(Don't say: She taught me how to make a bread).*

We say a piece of equipment, (NOT an equipment). Equipment is uncountable.

I bought a piece of equipment for my kitchen. *(Don't say: I bought an equipment for my kitchen).*

The surface area of a desk is occupied by a piece of equipment. *(Don't say: The surface area of a desk is occupied by an equipment).*

Describe a piece of equipment in your home. *(Don't say: Describe an equipment in your home).*

We say a piece of furniture, (NOT a furniture). Furniture is uncountable.

This sofa is a piece of furniture. *(Don't say: This sofa is a furniture).*

I bought a piece of furniture at the store. *(Don't say: I bought a furniture at the store).*

A chair is a piece of furniture for one person to sit on. *(Don't say: A chair is a furniture for one person to sit on).*

We say a piece of information, (NOT an information). Furniture is uncountable.

He brought me a piece of information. *(Don't say: He brought me an information).*

A rumor is a piece of information that has not been verified. *(Don't say: A rumor is an information that has not been verified).*

His telephone number is a piece of information. *(Don't say: His telephone number is an information).*

We say a piece of advice, (NOT an advice). Furniture is uncountable.

He gave me a piece of advice. *(Don't say: He gave me an advice).*

Let me give you a piece of advice. *(Don't say: Let me give you an advice).*

We say a fact, (NOT a knowledge). Knowledge is uncountable.

Baldness is a fact of life for men. *(Don't say: Baldness is a knowledge of life for men).*

I know for a fact that he was lying. *(Don't say: I know for a knowledge that he was lying).*

It is a fact that the Internet makes people's lives become more convenient. *(Don't say: It is a knowledge that the Internet makes people's lives become more convenient).*

We say a piece of luck, (NOT a luck). Luck is uncountable.

What a piece of luck! *(Don't say: What a luck!).*

A piece of luck happened to him. *(Don't say: A luck happened to him).*

We say piece of luggage, (NOT a luggage). Luggage is uncountable.

A piece of luggage carried on top of a coach. *(Don't say: A luggage carried on top of a coach).*

Wherever Peter goes, he leaves a piece of luggage behind. *(Don't say: Wherever Peter goes, he leaves a luggage behind).*

At the airport she realized that she had left a piece of luggage at home. *(Don't say: At the airport she realized that she had left a luggage at home).*

We say a piece of news, (NOT a news). News is uncountable.

I have a piece of news to tell you. *(Don't say: I have a news to tell you).*

I just read a piece of news about lung cancer on the website bbc.co.uk. *(Don't say: I just read a news about lung cancer on the website bbc.co.uk).*

We say an experiment, (NOT a research). Research is uncountable.

We carried out an experiment. *(Don't say: We carried out a research).*

A scientist performed an experiment on mice. *(Don't say: A scientist performed a research on mice).*

We say a piece of rubbish, (NOT a rubbish). Rubbish is uncountable.

He picked up a piece of rubbish and put it in the trash can. *(Don't say: He picked up a rubbish and put it in the trash can).*

We pick up a piece of rubbish floating by the roadside. *(Don't say: We pick up a rubbish floating by the roadside).*

Everyone can pick up a piece of rubbish every day. *(Don't say: Everyone can pick up a rubbish every day).*

We say a job, (NOT a work). Work is uncountable.

She has applied for a job at a department store. *(Don't say: She has applied for a work at a department store).*

Tom graduated last year but he still can't find a job. *(Don't say: Tom graduated last year but he still can't find a work).*

We say her hair is, (NOT her hair are). Hair is uncountable.

Her hair is very bright and golden. *(Don't say: Her hair are very bright and golden).*

His hair is naturally curly. *(Don't say: His hair are naturally curly).*

Her hair is very long. *(Don't say: Her hair are very long).*

We say good health, (NOT a good health). Health is uncountable.

I hope you are in good health. *(Don't say: I hope you are in a good health).*

My father has continued to enjoy good health in his old age. *(Don't say: My father has continued to enjoy a good health in his old age).*

We say some of the students/ some students, (NOT some of students).

Some of the students were late for school. *(Don't say: Some of students were late for school).*

Some students took their own handwritten notes on the lectures. *(Don't say: Some of students took their own handwritten notes on the lectures).*

Some of the workers tried to talk to their bosses about being treated more fairly. *(Don't say: ~~Some of workers~~ tried to talk to their bosses about being treated more fairly).*

Some workers do these tasks for her. *(Don't say: ~~Some of workers~~ do these tasks for her).*

We say each of my students/ each of the students/ each student, (NOT ~~each my students/ each of students~~).

Each of his students has a different assignment to complete. *(Don't say: ~~Each his students/ each of students~~ has a different assignment to complete).*

Each student has a different assignment to complete. *(Don't say: ~~Each of students~~ has a different assignment to complete).*

Each of the students has a different assignment to complete. *(Don't say: ~~Each of students~~ has a different assignment to complete).*

We use for (NOT ~~during~~) to say how long something lasts.

I have studied Japanese for 2 months. *(Don't say: I have studied Japanese ~~during~~ 2 months).*

I am on vacation for 3 weeks. *(Don't say: I am on vacation ~~during~~ 3 weeks).*

It hasn't rained for six months. *(Don't say: It hasn't rained ~~during~~ six months).*

We use how + adjective/adverb + subject + verb, (NOT ~~how + subject + verb + adjective/adverb~~).

How beautiful she is! *(Don't say: ~~How she is beautiful!~~).*

How excellent you are! *(Don't say: ~~How you are excellent!~~).*

How hot the weather is! *(Don't say: ~~How the weather is hot!~~).*

We use such a/an (+ adjective) + singular countable noun, (NOT ~~a/an~~ such (+ adjective) + singular countable noun).

It's such a beautiful day. *(Don't say: It's ~~a such~~ beautiful day).*

She's such a beautiful girl. *(Don't say: She's ~~a such~~ beautiful girl).*

I've never seen such a wonderful sunset. *(Don't say: I've never seen ~~a such~~ wonderful sunset).*

We use such (+ adjective) + uncountable/plural noun, (NOT such ~~a/an~~ (+ adjective) + uncountable/plural noun).

I've never seen such good things. *(Don't say: I've never seen such ~~a~~ good things).*

They are such nice people. *(Don't say: They are such ~~a~~ nice people).*

They're such friendly people that everyone likes them. *(Don't say: They're such ~~a~~ friendly people that everyone likes them).*

We use hope/expect + to infinitive (NOT hope/expect + ~~V-ing~~).

I expect to read this book. *(Don't say: I expect ~~reading~~ this book).*

I hope to pass the exam. *(Don't say: I hope ~~passing~~ the exam).*

She hopes to find a job in a hospital because she is a nurse. *(Don't say: She hopes ~~finding~~ a job in a hospital because she is a nurse).*

We say explain (something) to someone, (NOT ~~explain (something) someone~~).

I will explain the problem to you. *(Don't say: I will ~~explain you the problem~~).*

It was difficult to explain the problem to him. *(Don't say: It was difficult to ~~explain him the problem~~).*

Explain to me why he isn't here. *(Don't say: ~~Explain me~~ why he isn't here).*

Please explain to me why you were late last night. *(Don't say: Please ~~explain me~~ why you were late last night).*

We say drive/walk a long way to a place, (NOT drive/walk ~~far~~ to a place).

I have to drive a long way to my office. *(Don't say: I have to drive ~~far~~ to my office).*

I usually walk a long way to work. *(Don't say: I usually walk ~~far~~ to work).*

We say get somebody to do something, (NOT get somebody ~~do~~

something).

It is difficult for me to get her to pronounce French words properly. *(Don't say: It is difficult for me to get her pronounce French words properly)*.

I'll get her to phone you as soon as possible. *(Don't say: I'll get her phone you as soon as possible)*.

We say have/get something done, (NOT have/get something do/to do).

I had my house painted. *(Don't say: I had my house to paint/paint)*.

Tom had his car washed. *(Don't say: Tom had his car to wash/wash)*.

She is going to get her hair cut tomorrow. *(Don't say: She is going to get her hair to cut/cut tomorrow)*.

We say hear, (NOT hear to).

I heard footsteps behind me. *(Don't say: I heard to footsteps behind me)*.

Can you hear me? *(Don't say: Can you hear to me?)*.

Can you hear the rain? *(Don't say: Can you hear to the rain?)*.

We don't use progressive forms with "hear".

Can you hear me? *(Don't say: Are you hearing me?)*

Do you hear what I'm saying? *(Don't say: Are you hearing what I'm saying?)*

We say many + plural nouns, (NOT many + singular nouns).

How many brothers do you have? *(Don't say: How many brother do you have?)*.

How many children do you have? *(Don't say: How many child do you have?)*.

There are many tourists during the summer in Tokyo. *(Don't say: There are many tourist during the summer in Tokyo)*.

We say much + uncountable nouns, (NOT much + countable nouns).

I had spent too much money on my vacation.

How much money did you spend on your house?

We say If I were you, I would.., (NOT If I ~~was~~ you, I ~~will~~).

If I were you, I would study harder. *(Don't say: If I ~~was~~ you, I ~~will~~ study harder).*

If I were you, I would book a flight now. *(Don't say: If I ~~was~~ you, I ~~will~~ book a flight now).*

If I were you, I would give up smoking. *(Don't say: If I ~~was~~ you, I ~~will~~ give up smoking).*

To talk about the future we use if only + subject + would + Vo, (NOT if only + subject + ~~will~~ + Vo).

If only Tom would save money. *(Don't say: If only Tom ~~will~~ save money).*

If only she would sell me her car this week, I would give her $2000 more. *(Don't say: If only she would sell me her car this week, I ~~will~~ give her $2000 more).*

If only he would listen to me! *(Don't say: If only he ~~will~~ listen to me!).*

To talk about the present we use if only + subject + V2/V-ed, (NOT if only + subject + ~~V(s/es)~~).

If only she knew the truth. *(Don't say: If only she ~~knows~~ the truth).*

If only I learnt to swim. *(Don't say: If only I ~~learn~~ to swim).*

If only Mary heard what they say about her behind her back. *(Don't say: If only Mary ~~hears~~ what they say about her behind her back).*

To talk about the past we use if only + subject + had + V3, (NOT if only + subject + ~~V2/V-ed~~).

If only she had been at the meeting. *(Don't say: If only she ~~was~~ at the meeting).*

If only I had been sick tomorrow instead, I would have been happier. *(Don't say: If only I ~~were~~ sick tomorrow instead, I would have been happier).*

If only she had listened to what her friends had been telling her. *(Don't say: If only she ~~listened~~ to what her friends had been telling her).*

We say He said that he was tired, (NOT He said that ~~I~~ was tired or He said that he ~~is~~ tired).

He said that he was tired. *(Don't say: He said that ~~I~~ was tired or He said that he ~~is~~ tired).*

Mary said that she was very happy. *(Don't say: Mary said that ~~I~~ was very happy or Mary said that she ~~is~~ very happy).*

We say He said that he would, (NOT He said that he ~~will~~).

Mary said that she would come back here next week. *(Don't say: Mary said that she ~~will~~ come back here next week).*

Tom said that he would start jogging again next week. *(Don't say: Tom said that he ~~will~~ start jogging again next week).*

We say try not to, (NOT ~~try to not~~).

He tried not to show his surprise. *(Don't say: He ~~tried to not~~ show his surprise).*

I tried not to laugh. *(Don't say: I ~~tried to not~~ laugh).*

She tried not to look into his eyes. *(Don't say: She ~~tried to not~~ look into his eyes).*

We say had better + Vo, (NOT had better + ~~To infinitive/V-ing~~).

We'd better go now before the traffic gets too bad. *(Don't say: We'd better ~~to go~~ now before the traffic gets too bad).*

You'd better tell him everything. *(Don't say: You'd better ~~to tell~~ him everything).*

We say finish/admit/avoid/delay/postpone + V-ing, (NOT finish + ~~To infinitive~~).

I've finished reading this book. *(Don't say: I've finished ~~to read~~ this book).*

He admitted having stolen the money. *(Don't say: He admitted ~~to have~~ stolen the money).*

Tom avoided doing his homework. *(Don't say: Tom avoided ~~to do~~ his homework).*

Mary delayed writing her essay. *(Don't say: Mary delayed ~~to write~~ her essay).*

Don't postpone doing what you love. *(Don't say: Don't postpone ~~to do~~ what you love)*.

We say stop/prevent someone (from) doing something, (NOT stop/prevent someone ~~to do~~ something).

She couldn't stop her baby from crying. *(Don't say: She couldn't stop her baby ~~to cry~~)*.

I stopped her from killing herself. *(Don't say: I stopped her ~~to kill~~ herself)*.

I can't prevent him from drinking. *(Don't say: I can't prevent him ~~to kill~~)*.

She wants to prevent him from getting sick. *(Don't say: She wants to prevent him ~~to get~~ sick)*.

We say be used to + V-ing, (NOT be used to + ~~Vo~~).

I am used to drinking coffee every morning. *(Don't say: I am used ~~to drink~~ coffee every morning)*.

She is used to living alone. *(Don't say: She is used ~~to live~~ alone)*.

We say be accustomed to + V-ing, (NOT be accustomed to + ~~Vo~~).

She's accustomed to sleeping in a room without air conditioning. *(Don't say: She's accustomed ~~to sleep~~ in a room without air conditioning)*.

He is accustomed to eating this food. *(Don't say: He is accustomed ~~to eat~~ this food)*.

Lie – lay – lain **means** to be in a flat or horizontal position in which your body is on a surface such as a bed or a floor.

Lay – laid – laid **means** to put someone or something down gently or carefully.

He just wants to lie in bed all day. *(Don't say: He just wants to ~~lay~~ in bed all day)*.

She did nothing but lie in bed all day. *(Don't say: She did nothing but ~~laid~~ in bed all day)*.

Now the exams are over, so I can lie in bed all day. *(Don't say: Now the exams are over, so I can ~~lay~~ in bed all day).*

I lay the book on the table. *(Don't say: I ~~lie~~ the book on the table).*

I lay the folders on the desk. *(Don't say: I ~~lie~~ the folders on the desk).*

We use the least + uncountable nouns

We use the fewest + countable nouns

She drank the least amount of milk of anyone there. *(Don't say: She drank ~~the fewest~~ amount of milk of anyone there).*

She tries to spend the least amount of time possible in the kitchen. *(Don't say: She tries to spend ~~the fewest~~ amount of time possible in the kitchen).*

Peter made the fewest mistakes in the English test. *(Don't say: Peter made ~~the least~~ mistakes in the English test).*

The safest place when driving is the place with the fewest cars. *(Don't say: The safest place when driving is the place with ~~the least~~ cars).*

We say work as a salesman, (NOT work ~~like~~ a salesman).

He works as a salesman. *(Don't say: He works ~~like~~ a salesman).*

Lucy works as a nurse in the local hospital. *(Don't say: Lucy works ~~like~~ a nurse in the local hospital).*

My father works as a teacher. *(Don't say: My father works ~~like~~ a teacher).*

We say wait for a long time, (NOT wait ~~long~~).

I waited for a long time in the rain for the bus. *(Don't say: I waited ~~long~~ time in the rain for the bus).*

He has waited for a long time to have a chance to show his talent. *(Don't say: He has waited ~~long~~ time to have a chance to show his talent).*

We say take a long time, (NOT take ~~long~~).

It took a long time for him to write the essay. *(Don't say: It ~~took long~~ for him to write the essay).*

The film took a long time to watch. *(Don't say: The film took long to watch).*

It takes a long time to learn Chinese. *(Don't say: It takes long to learn Chinese).*

We say advice, (NOT advices). Advice is an uncountable noun.

He gave me some good advice. *(Don't say: He gave me some good advices).*

She asked her father for some good advice. *(Don't say: She asked her father for some good advices).*

We say information, (NOT informations). Information is an uncountable noun.

I need some information. *(Don't say: I need some informations).*

He has some information for me about flights to London. *(Don't say: He has some informations for me about flights to London).*

We say furniture, (NOT furnitures). Furniture is an uncountable noun.

I need to buy some furniture. *(Don't say: I need to buy some furnitures).*

My father used to make his own furniture. *(Don't say: My father used to make his own furnitures).*

We say damage, (NOT damages). Damage is an uncountable noun.

The storm did not cause much damage. *(Don't say: The storm did not cause much damages).*

Did the accident cause any damage? *(Don't say: Did the accident cause any damages?).*

We say work, (NOT works). Work is an uncountable noun means *a job or task need to be done.*

Taking care of a baby is hard work. *(Don't say: Taking care of a baby is hard works).*

I have so much work to do now. *(Don't say: I have so much works to do now).*

We say fish, (NOT ~~fishes~~). Damage is an uncountable noun.

There are a lot of fish in this lake. *(Don't say: There are a lot of ~~fishes~~ in this lake).*

He ate a lot of fish. *(Don't say: He ate a lot of ~~fishes~~).*

We say fruit, (NOT ~~fruits~~). Fruit is an uncountable noun.

Would you like some fruit for dessert? *(Don't say: Would you like some ~~fruits~~ for dessert?).*

Oranges, bananas, pears, and apples are all types of fruit. *(Don't say: Oranges, bananas, pears, and apples are all types of ~~fruits~~).*

We say knowledge, (NOT ~~knowledges~~). Knowledge is an uncountable noun.

She has a good knowledge of Japanese. *(Don't say: She has a good ~~knowledges~~ of Japanese).*

My father likes reading because he likes to broaden his knowledge. *(Don't say: My father likes reading because he likes to broaden his ~~knowledges~~).*

We say data, (NOT ~~datas~~). Data is an uncountable noun.

Most of the data are new. *(Don't say: Most of the ~~datas~~ are new).*

The data was collected by various researchers over a period of three months. *(Don't say: The ~~datas~~ was collected by various researchers over a period of three months).*

We say evidence, (NOT ~~evidences~~). Evidence is an uncountable noun.

The police assembled a lot of evidence against her. *(Don't say: The police assembled a lot of ~~evidences~~ against her).*

There is a lot of evidence against him. *(Don't say: There is a lot of ~~evidences~~ against him).*

We say money + singular verb, (NOT money + ~~plural verb~~).

All his money is spent on his girlfriend and drugs. *(Don't say: All his money are spent on his girlfriend and drugs).*

All her money is spent on shoes and clothes. *(Don't say: All her money are spent on shoes and clothes).*

We say the number of + plural noun + singular verb, (NOT the number of + plural noun + plural verb).

The number of students in the class is eighteen. *(Don't say: The number of students in the class are eighteen).*

The number of houses is increasing significantly. *(Don't say: The number of houses are increasing significantly).*

We say a number of + plural nouns + plural verbs, (NOT a number of + plural nouns + singular verbs).

A number of students are absent today. *(Don't say: A number of students is absent today).*

A number of houses are rented. *(Don't say: A number of houses is rented).*

We say their lives, (NOT their life).

Because of that virus, many people lost their lives. *(Don't say: Because of that virus, many people lost their life).*

Many people lost their lives in the battle. *(Don't say: Many people lost their life in the battle).*

We say their behaviors, (NOT their behavior).

Not all children are able to control their behaviors. *(Don't say: Not all children are able to control their behavior).*

I began to observe their behaviors. *(Don't say: I began to observe their behavior).*

We say to do something very well, (NOT to do something very good).

He plays guitar very well. *(Don't say: He plays guitar very good).*

She speaks English very well. *(Don't say: She speaks English very good).*

We say a white brand new car, (NOT a brand new white car).

My father just bought a white brand new car yesterday. *(Don't say: My father just bought a brand new white car yesterday).*

Tom's mother gave him a black brand new watch on his birthday. *(Don't say: Tom's mother gave him a brand new black watch on his birthday).*

We say the party was very fun, (NOT the party was very funny).

The party was very fun and exciting. *(Don't say: The party was very funny and exciting).*

Our trip was very fun and relaxing. *(Don't say: Our trip was very funny and relaxing).*

We say at 7pm, (NOT on 7pm).

I left work at 6 pm and arrived home at 7 pm. *(Don't say: I left work at 6 pm and arrived home on 7 pm).*

The meeting that will be held on Monday at 9 am. *(Don't say: The meeting that will be held on Monday at 9 am).*

We say on Saturday, (NOT at Saturday).

I usually go swimming on Saturday. *(Don't say: I usually go swimming at Saturday).*

We visited our grandparents on Monday. *(Don't say: We visited our grandparents at Monday).*

We say on Sunday morning/afternoon/evening, (NOT in Sunday morning/afternoon/evening).

I go to church on Sunday morning. *(Don't say: I go to church in Sunday morning).*

My mom and I usually go shopping on Sunday afternoon. *(Don't say: My mom and I usually go shopping in Sunday afternoon).*

We usually go to the cinema on Sunday evening. *(Don't say: We usually go to the cinema in Sunday evening).*

We say in May, (NOT ~~on~~ May).

I will visit my sister in May. *(Don't say: I will visit my sister ~~on~~ May).*

She will graduate in August 2014. *(Don't say: She will graduate ~~on~~ August 2014).*

We say in the winter, (NOT ~~on~~ the winter).

We like to go skiing in the winter. *(Don't say: We like to go skiing ~~on~~ the winter).*

I went to Japan in the summer of 2012. *(Don't say: I went to Japan ~~on~~ the summer of 2012).*

We say on the bus, (NOT ~~in~~ the bus).

I sat next to her on the bus. *(Don't say: I sat next to her ~~in~~ the bus).*

I am on the bus. *(Don't say: I am ~~in~~ the bus).*

We say call someone, (NOT ~~call to~~ someone).

He called me when he got home. *(Don't say: He ~~called to~~ me when he got home).*

She only called me when she needed some help. *(Don't say: She only ~~called to~~ me when she needed some help).*

We say when someone does something, (NOT when someone ~~will do~~ something).

When I arrive at the airport, I will phone you. *(Don't say: When I ~~will arrive~~ at the airport, I will phone you).*

I'll call you when I get home. *(Don't say: I'll call you when I ~~will get~~ home).*

We say for four years, (NOT ~~since~~ four years).

I have worked here for four years. *(Don't say: I have worked here ~~since~~ four years).*

He's been married for six years. *(Don't say: He's been married ~~since~~ six years).*

We say are you thirsty? (NOT ~~do~~ you thirsty?)

Are you tired? *(Don't say: ~~Do~~ you tired?)*.

Are you sad? *(Don't say: ~~Do~~ you sad?)*.

We say my glasses, (NOT my ~~glass~~).

I'm looking for my glasses. *(Don't say: I'm looking for my ~~glass~~)*.

I lost my glasses. *(Don't say: I lost my ~~glass~~)*.

We say be successful, (NOT be ~~success~~).

Tom is successful in his love and job. *(Don't say: Tom is ~~success~~ in his love and job)*.

This police officer is successful in catching the criminals in his city. *(Don't say: This police officer is ~~success~~ in catching the criminals in his city)*.

We say do sports, (NOT ~~make~~ sports).

Do you like doing sports? *(Don't say: Do you like ~~make~~ sports?)*.

In his free time, he likes doing sports. *(Don't say: In his free time, he likes ~~make~~ sports)*.

We say a tall man, (NOT a ~~high~~ man).

Her father is a tall man. *(Don't say: Her father is a ~~high~~ man)*.

He is tall and strong. *(Don't say: He is ~~high~~ and strong)*.

We say younger brother/ little brother, (NOT ~~small~~ brother).

He is my younger brother. *(Don't say: He is my ~~small~~ brother)*.

He is my little brother. *(Don't say: He is my ~~small~~ brother)*.

We say elder brother/ older brother, (NOT ~~bigger~~ brother).

He is poor while his elder brother is rich. *(Don't say: He is poor while his ~~bigger~~ brother is rich)*.

He's her older brother. *(Don't say: He's her ~~bigger~~ brother).*

We say a university, (NOT ~~an~~ university).

She studies at a university in London. *(Don't say: She studies at ~~an~~ university in London).*

Her dream is to go to a university in America. *(Don't say: Her dream is to go to ~~an~~ university in America).*

We say be disappointed in/with someone, (NOT be disappointed ~~about~~ someone).

I'm disappointed in him - I really thought I could trust him! *(Don't say: I'm disappointed ~~about~~ him - I really thought I could trust him).*

Her parents were disappointed with her. *(Don't say: Her parents were disappointed ~~about~~ her).*

We say on foot, (NOT ~~by~~ foot).

The mall is not very far, let's go on foot. *(Don't say: The mall is not very far, let's go ~~by foot~~).*

I go to school on foot every day. *(Don't say: I go to school ~~by foot~~ every day).*

We say come to an event, (NOT ~~come an event~~).

How many people came to the meeting today? *(Don't say: How many people came the meeting today?).*

Will you come to the party tonight? *(Don't say: Will you come the party tonight?).*

We say he and I, (NOT he and ~~me~~).

He and I are going to visit my sister. *(Don't say: He and ~~me~~ are going to visit my sister).*

She and I went to dinner. *(Don't say: She and ~~me~~ went to dinner).*

We say children, (NOT ~~childrens~~).

How many children do you have? *(Don't say: How many ~~childrens~~ do you have?).*

I have 2 children, a boy and a girl. *(Don't say: I have 2 ~~childrens~~, a boy and a girl).*

We say can't hear anything, (NOT can't hear ~~nothing~~).

I'm listening but I can't hear anything. *(Don't say: I'm listening but I can't hear ~~nothing~~).*

I can't hear anything because of the noise. *(Don't say: I can't hear ~~nothing~~ because of the noise).*

We say crash into, (NOT ~~crash~~).

The car crashed into the house. *(Don't say: The car crashed the house).*

The truck crashed into a tree. *(Don't say: The truck crashed a tree).*

We say I like/love, (NOT ~~I am liking/loving~~).

I like playing the guitar. *(Don't say: I ~~am liking~~ playing the guitar).*

I love playing football. *(Don't say: I ~~am loving~~ playing football).*

We say must do something, (NOT must ~~to do~~ something).

You must do your homework. *(Don't say: You must ~~to do~~ your homework).*

I must go now. *(Don't say: I must ~~to go~~ now).*

We say look/seem/feel + adjective, (NOT look/seem/feel + ~~adverb~~).

She looks sad. *(Don't say: she looks ~~sadly~~)*

He seems happy in his new job. *(Don't say: He seems ~~happily~~ in his new job).*

Tom feels happy when he can spend time with his family. *(Don't say: Tom feels ~~happily~~ when he can spend time with his family).*

She feels happy and sad at the same time. *(Don't say: She feels ~~happily~~ and ~~sadly~~ at the same time).*

We say do business, (NOT ~~make~~ business).

Let's do business. *(Don't say: Let's ~~make~~ business).*

It's my pleasure to do business with you. *(Don't say: It's my pleasure to ~~make~~ business with you).*

They've been doing a lot of business in Europe recently. *(Don't say: They've been ~~making~~ a lot of business in Europe recently).*

We say go home, (NOT ~~go to~~ home).

Let's go home now. *(Don't say: Let's ~~go to~~ home now).*

I felt tired, and I went home early. *(Don't say: I felt tired, and I ~~went to~~ home early).*

We say anxious about something, (NOT ~~anxious for~~ something).

She is anxious about her father's health. *(Don't say: She is ~~anxious for~~ her father's health).*

Tom is anxious about his upcoming surgery. *(Don't say: Tom is ~~anxious for~~ his upcoming surgery).*

We say anxious for somebody, (NOT ~~anxious about~~ somebody).

We are very anxious for him to reach home in time. *(Don't say: We are very ~~anxious about~~ him to reach home in time).*

Her father was anxious for her to leave. *(Don't say: Her father was ~~anxious about~~ her to leave).*

We say be good/excellent at something, (NOT be good/excellent ~~with~~ something).

He is good at playing the guitar. *(Don't say: He is good ~~with~~ playing the guitar).*

My father is excellent at drawing. *(Don't say: My father is excellent ~~with~~ drawing).*

We say be/get married to, (NOT be/get married ~~with~~).

Tom was married to Mary last week. *(Don't say: Tom was married ~~with~~ Mary last week).*

I got married to Lucy when I was 22. *(Don't say: I got married ~~with~~ Lucy when I was 22).*

We say be proud of, (NOT be proud ~~about~~).

She was proud of her clever son. *(Don't say: She was proud ~~about~~ her clever son).*

We are proud of you. *(Don't say: We are proud ~~about~~ you).*

We say be satisfied with, (NOT be satisfied ~~about~~).

She is not satisfied with her English ability. *(Don't say: She is not satisfied ~~about~~ her English ability).*

He is not satisfied with the results of the exams. *(Don't say: He is not satisfied ~~about~~ the results of the exams).*

We say everyone + singular verb, (NOT everyone + ~~plural verb~~).

Everyone needs help from other people. *(Don't say: Everyone ~~need~~ help from other people).*

Everyone is happy. *(Don't say: Everyone ~~are~~ happy).*

We say every of + plural noun + singular verb, (NOT every of + plural noun + ~~plural verb~~).

Every of my friends likes horror films. *(Don't say: Every of my friends ~~like~~ horror films).*

Every of my friends studies English. *(Don't say: Every of my friends ~~study~~ English).*

We say near my school, (NOT near ~~to~~ my school).

There is a bank near my school. *(Don't say: There is a bank ~~near to~~ my school).*

She keeps most of her money at the bank near her office. *(Don't say: She keeps most of her money at the bank ~~near to~~ her office).*

We say make a sandwich, (NOT ~~do~~ a sandwich or ~~cook~~ a sandwich).

Will you make a sandwich for me? *(Don't say: Will you ~~do/cook~~ a sandwich for me?).*

I made a sandwich for lunch. *(Don't say: I ~~did/ cooked~~ a sandwich for lunch).*

We say have breakfast, have lunch, have dinner, (NOT have ~~a~~ breakfast, have ~~a~~ lunch, have ~~a~~ dinner).

Sit down and have breakfast with us. *(Don't say: Sit down and ~~have a breakfast~~ with us).*

What time do you usually have lunch? *(Don't say: What time do you usually ~~have a lunch?~~).*

Would you like to have dinner with me? *(Don't say: Would you like to ~~have a dinner~~ with me?).*

We say are you married? , (NOT ~~have~~ you married? Or ~~do~~ you married?).

Is she married? *(Don't say: ~~Has/does~~ she married?).*

Is Tom married? *(Don't say: ~~Has/does~~ Tom married?).*

We say do you feel? , (NOT ~~are~~ you feel?).

Do you feel secure about the future? *(Don't say: ~~Are~~ you feel secure about the future?).*

Do you feel better? *(Don't say: ~~Are~~ you feel better?).*

We say he/she lives in, (NOT he/she ~~live~~ in).

She lives in London. *(Don't say: She ~~live~~ in London).*

He lives in New York. *(Don't say: He ~~live~~ in New York).*

We say does he/she have?, (NOT does he/she ~~has?~~).

Does she have any children? *(Don't say: ~~Does she has~~ any children?).*

Does he have a girlfriend? *(Don't say: ~~Does he has~~ a girlfriend?).*

We say have you bought a car, (NOT ~~has~~ you bought a car?).

Have you read this book already? *(Don't say: ~~Has you~~ read this book already?).*

Have you visited Sydney? *(Don't say: Has you visited Sydney?).*

We say has she/he bought a car?, (NOT have she/he bought a car?).

Has Mary told you the good news, yet? *(Don't say: Have Mary told you the good news, yet?).*

Has Tom got a computer? *(Don't say: Have Tom got a computer?).*

We say he and she are, (NOT he and she is).

He and she are siblings. *(Don't say: He and she is siblings).*

He and she are going out together. *(Don't say: He and she is going out together).*

We say watch TV, (NOT see or look at TV).

My father likes to watch TV. *(Don't say: My father likes to see/look at TV).*

Her mother doesn't let her watch TV after 11:00 p.m. *(Don't say: Her mother doesn't let her see/look at TV after 11:00 p.m).*

We say didn't + Vo, (NOT didn't + V2/V-ed).

I didn't play badminton yesterday. *(Don't say: I didn't played badminton yesterday).*

I didn't talk to him a lot last night. *(Don't say: I didn't talked to him a lot last night).*

We say someone has done something for 2 years, (NOT someone did something for 2 years).

She has studied English for 2 years. *(Don't say: She studied English for 2 years).*

He has played football for 5 years. *(Don't say: He played football for 5 years).*

We say someone has done something since…, (NOT someone did something since…).

Tom has studied English since he was six years old. *(Don't say: Tom studied English since he was six years old).*

I have played the guitar since I was 20. *(Don't say: I played the guitar since I was 20).*

We say 2 days ago, (NOT 2 days before).

Tom and Mary got married 2 days ago. *(Don't say: Tom and Mary got married 2 days before).*

I had dinner with him three days ago. *(Don't say: I had dinner with him three days before).*

We say someone did something yesterday/last week, (NOT someone has done something yesterday/last week).

I bought a car yesterday. *(Don't say: I have bought a car yesterday).*

I had dinner with Mary last week. *(Don't say: I have had dinner with Mary last week).*

We say must/have to + Vo, (NOT must/have to + V2/V-ed).

I was very thirsty. I had to drink something. *(Don't say: I had to drank something).*

I was very tired. I must get some rest. *(Don't say: I must got some rest).*

We say return to, (NOT return back to).

We didn't know what to do, so we returned to our hotel. *(Don't say: We didn't know what to do, so we returned back to our hotel).*

I finished reading the novel and returned it to Peter. *(Don't say: I finished reading the novel and returned it back to Peter).*

We say in my opinion, (NOT according to me).

In my opinion, he is correct. *(Don't say: according to me, he is correct).*

In my opinion, Lucy is old enough to know what she did was wrong. *(Don't say: according to me, Lucy is old enough to know what she did was wrong).*

We say except someone, (NOT except for someone).

Nobody knows we are here except her. *(Don't say: Nobody knows we are here except for her).*

Everyone arrived on time except Tom. *(Don't say: Everyone arrived on time except for Tom).*

We say finish something by Friday, (NOT finish something until Friday).

I have to finish the essay by Friday. *(Don't say: I have to finish the essay until Friday).*

I have to finish the homework by 7 pm. *(Don't say: I have to finish the homework until 7 pm).*

We say a fast car, fast food, (NOT a quick car, quick food).

My brother has a fast car. *(Don't say: My brother has a quick car).*

My son likes to eat fast food such as hamburgers, fried chicken, and pizza. *(Don't say: My son likes to eat quick food...).*

We say a quick meal, (NOT a fast meal).

We had a quick meal in the restaurant. *(Don't say: We had a fast meal in the restaurant).*

We had a quick meal before a movie. *(Don't say: We had a fast meal before a movie).*

We say powerful engine, (NOT strong engine).

This is a new car with a powerful engine. *(Don't say: This is a new car with a strong engine).*

I would like to possess a motor vehicle with a powerful engine. *(Don't say: I would like to possess a motor vehicle with a strong engine).*

We say someone is injured, (NOT someone is damaged).

He was injured in the accident. *(Don't say: He was damaged in the accident).*

Fortunately, nobody was injured in the car accident. *(Don't say: Fortunately, nobody was ~~damaged~~ in the car accident).*

Tom injured his arm and stayed in hospital after the car accident. *(Don't say: Tom ~~damaged~~ his arm and stayed in hospital after the car accident).*

We say something is damaged, (NOT something is ~~injured~~).

The house was damaged by the storm. *(Don't say: The house was ~~injured~~ by the storm).*

The building was damaged by the fire. *(Don't say: The building was ~~injured~~ by the fire).*

Tom's house was badly damaged in the fire. *(Don't say: Tom's house was badly ~~injured~~ in the fire).*

We say to rob someone or an organization, (NOT to ~~steal~~ someone or an organization).

He robbed the bank. *(Don't say: He ~~stole~~ the bank).*

He robbed an elderly man. *(Don't say: He ~~stole~~ an elderly man).*

We say to steal something, (NOT to ~~rob~~ something).

He stole money from his parents. *(Don't say: He ~~robbed~~ money from his parents).*

He was arrested because he stole a car. *(Don't say: He was arrested because he ~~robbed~~ a car).*

We say the latest news, (NOT the ~~last~~ news).

Have you heard the latest news? *(Don't say: Have you heard the ~~last~~ news?).*

I keep up to date with the latest news via the smartphone. *(Don't say: I keep up to date with the ~~last~~ news via the smartphone).*

We say speak a language, (NOT ~~talk~~ a language).

Do you speak English? *(Don't say: Do you ~~talk~~ English?).*

I can speak English, French and Chinese. *(Don't say: I can ~~talk~~ English, French and Chinese).*

We say reject an idea/a suggestion, (NOT ~~refuse~~ an idea/a suggestion).

They quickly rejected his idea. *(Don't say: They quickly ~~refused~~ his idea).*

She rejected my suggestion as impractical. *(Don't say: She ~~refused~~ my suggestion as impractical).*

We say refuse an invitation/offer, (NOT ~~reject~~ an invitation/offer).

He refused my invitation. *(Don't say: He rejected my invitation).*

Mary refused his offer of working in New York for a year. *(Don't say: Mary rejected his offer of working in New York for a year).*

We say very happy, (NOT ~~absolutely~~ happy).

He was very happy about his unexpected promotion. *(Don't say: He was ~~absolutely~~ happy about his unexpected promotion).*

We are very happy about the birth of our new baby. *(Don't say: We are ~~absolutely~~ happy about the birth of our new baby).*

We say be under a lot of/considerable pressure, (be under ~~high~~ pressure).

She has been under a lot of pressure lately. *(Don't say: She has been under ~~high~~ pressure lately).*

He was under considerable pressure at times. *(Don't say: He was under ~~high~~ pressure at times).*

We say someone wants to do something, (NOT someone ~~is wanting to~~ do something).

I'm hungry now. I want to eat something. *(Don't say: I ~~am wanting~~ to eat something).*

I want to see you now. *(Don't say: I ~~am wanting~~ to see you now).*

We use "anything" is used in negative sentences. (NOT ~~everything~~).

He didn't remember anything. *(Don't say: He didn't remember ~~everything~~).*

I can't do anything else. *(Don't say: I can't do ~~everything~~ else).*

We use "everything" is used in positive sentences. (NOT ~~anything~~).

I bought everything at the mall. *(Don't say: I bought ~~anything~~ at the mall).*

He has lost everything. *(Don't say: He has lost ~~anything~~).*

We say an excellent resume. (NOT ~~excellent resume~~).

This is an excellent resume. *(Don't say: This is excellent resume).*

This is an example of a physical change. *(Don't say: This is example of a physical change).*

She is a beautiful girl. *(Don't say: She is beautiful girl).*

We say secure/safe place. (NOT ~~security~~ place).

Keep your passport in a secure place. *(Don't say: Keep your passport in a ~~security~~ place).*

They found a safe place to take shelter from the storm. *(Don't say: They found a ~~security~~ place to take shelter from the storm).*

We say that pair of shoes is. (NOT that pair of shoes ~~are~~).

That pair of shoes is not new. *(Don't say: That pair of shoes ~~are~~ not new).*

That pair of shoes is a bit too expensive. *(Don't say: That pair of shoes ~~are~~ a bit too expensive).*

We say my father as well as my brothers is. (NOT my father as well as my brothers ~~are~~).

My father as well as my brothers is enjoying the party. *(Don't say: My father as well as my brothers ~~are~~ enjoying the party).*

My brother as well as my sisters is going to London next summer. *(Don't say: My brother as well as my sisters ~~are~~ going to London next summer).*

We say Diabetes is. (NOT Diabetes ~~are~~).

Diabetes is a dangerous disease. *(Don't say: Diabetes ~~are~~ a dangerous disease).*

Arthritis is most commonly seen in adults over the age of 65. *(Don't say: Arthritis are most commonly seen in adults over the age of 65).*

Measles is most commonly seen in children below 5-6 years. *(Don't say: Measles are most commonly seen in children below 5-6 years).*

We say mathematics is. (NOT mathematics are).

Mathematics is my brother's strength. *(Don't say: Mathematics are my brother's strength).*

Economics is a very difficult subject. *(Don't say: Economics are a very difficult subject).*

We say 50 dollars is. (NOT 50 dollars are).

The book which costs 50 dollars is put on the desks. *(Don't say: The book which costs 50 dollars are put on the desks).*

A million dollars is more than enough to buy a house. *(Don't say: A million dollars are more than enough to buy a house).*

Her wedding ring is worth a million dollars. *(Don't say: Her wedding ring are worth a million dollars).*

We say 30 minutes is. (NOT 30 minutes are).

30 minutes is not enough time for her to write an essay. *(Don't say: 30 minutes are not enough time for her to write an essay).*

2 hours is not enough for our event. *(Don't say: 2 hours are not enough for our event).*

We say 20 kilometers is. (NOT 20 kilometers are).

20 kilometers is a long distance. *(Don't say: 20 kilometers are a long distance).*

Five kilometers is too far for the child to walk. *(Don't say: Five kilometers are too far for the child to walk).*

We say some of + plural noun + plural verb, (NOT some of + plural noun + singular verb).

Some of the students are so excited about the course. *(Don't say: Some of the students ~~is~~ so excited about the course).*

Some of the cakes are not ready. *(Don't say: Some of the cakes ~~is~~ not ready).*

We say some of + singular noun + singular verb, (NOT some of + plural noun + ~~plural verb~~).

Some of the money is given to a poor man. *(Don't say: Some of the money ~~are~~ given to a poor man).*

Some of the water is evaporated. *(Don't say: Some of the water ~~are~~ evaporated).*

"Almost" is an adverb means *nearly, approximately*

"Most" is an adjective means *the majority, the largest part, nearly all of*

Most students study hard. *(Don't say: ~~Almost~~ students study hard).*

Most people would like to travel around the world. *(Don't say: ~~Almost~~ people would like to travel around the world).*

Tom almost failed the exam. *(Don't say: Tom ~~most~~ failed the exam).*

My father is almost eighty years old. *(Don't say: My father is ~~most~~ eighty years old).*

We say someone's thought, (NOT someone's ~~thinking~~).

Children's behaviors and thoughts. *(Don't say: Children's behaviors and ~~thinking~~).*

According to her thought, all violence is evil. *(Don't say: According to her ~~thinking~~, all violence is evil).*

We use inversion with seldom or rarely.

Rarely do we go to the movies these days. *(Don't say: Rarely we go to the movies these days).*

Rarely does she eats meat. *(Don't say: ~~Rarely she~~ eats meat).*

Seldom do I have a dream. *(Don't say: ~~Seldom I~~ have a dream).*

We say the most effective way, (NOT the ~~best~~ effective way).

The most effective way to improve your English skills is to study regularly. *(Don't say: The ~~best~~ effective way to improve your English skills is to study regularly).*

The most effective method to develop and improve your health is daily exercise. *(Don't say: The ~~best~~ effective method to develop and improve your health is daily exercise).*

We say farmer, (NOT ~~famer~~).

They are farmers, who keep herds of cattle and goats. *(Don't say: They are ~~famers~~, who keep herds of cattle and goats).*

Her father is a farmer. *(Don't say: Her father is a ~~famer~~).*

We say negative influences, (NOT ~~bad~~ influences).

Pesticides have many negative influences on people's health. *(Don't say: Pesticides have many ~~bad~~ influences on people's health).*

Poverty has many negative influences on families. *(Don't say: Poverty has many ~~bad~~ influences on families).*

Smoking has many negative influences on oral cavity. *(Don't say: Smoking has many ~~bad~~ influences on oral cavity).*

The plural form of "offspring" is "offspring", (NOT ~~offsprings~~).

Conflicts between parents and offspring. *(Don't say: Conflicts between parents and ~~offsprings~~).*

Nowadays, aging parents are less likely to live together with their offspring. *(Don't say: Nowadays, aging parents are less likely to live together with their ~~offsprings~~).*

We say be lack of + noun, (NOT be ~~lack + noun~~).

Her mother's problem is lack of sleep. *(Don't say: Her mother's problem is ~~lack sleep~~).*

His only problem is lack of confidence. *(Don't say: His only problem is ~~lack confidence~~).*

We say lack + noun, (NOT lack of + noun).

He lacks money to buy a house. (Don't say: He lacks of money to buy a house).

They lack money to buy food. (Don't say: They lack of money to buy food).

They lack food to feed themselves and their children. (Don't say: They lack of food to feed themselves and their children).

We say be/feel scared, (NOT be/feel scare).

She is scared of going out alone at night. (Don't say: She is scare of going out alone at night).

She feels scared to drive on the road by herself. (Don't say: She feels scare to drive on the road by herself).

The blind, the deaf, the mute, the dead, the injured, the old, the poor, the rich, the unemployed, the jobless, the young, the mentally ill are always plural.

The rich are not always happy. (Don't say: The rich is not always happy).

The rich are usually powerful. (Don't say: The rich is usually powerful).

The poor are not always unhappy. (Don't say: The poor is not always unhappy).

The unemployed are still increasing. (Don't say: The unemployed is still increasing).

The young don't usually plan ahead. (Don't say: The young doesn't usually plan ahead).

The injured are still in hospital in a critical condition. (Don't say: The injured is still in hospital in a critical condition).

We say over the last five years, (NOT during five years up to now).

I've used this car often over the last five years. (Don't say: I've used this car often during five years up to now).

She's been getting better and better at Japanese over the last three years.

(Don't say: She's been getting better and better at Japanese during three years up to now).

We say contribute to something/V-ing, (NOT contribute to + Vo).

He would like to contribute to arresting that man. *(Don't say: He would like to contribute to arrest that man).*

Technology has contributed to improving our lives. *(Don't say: Technology has contributed to improve our lives).*

We say consumers' health, (NOT consumer's health).

There are many negative effects of fast food on consumers' health. *(Don't say: There are many negative effects of fast food on consumer's health).*

Workers' compensation insurance. *(Don't say: Worker's compensation insurance).*

We say unhealthy food, (NOT harmful food).

People should keep themselves from consuming unhealthy food. *(Don't say: People should keep themselves from consuming harmful food).*

We should not buy or eat unhealthy food. *(Don't say: We should not buy or eat harmful food).*

We say detrimental/devastating effects, (NOT harmful effects).

The sun's detrimental/devastating effects on skin. *(Don't say: The sun's harmful effects on skin).*

Pesticides have detrimental/devastating effects on people's health and the environment. *(Don't say: Pesticides have harmful effects on people's health and the environment).*

The drought has had detrimental/devastating effects. *(Don't say: The drought has had harmful effects).*

We say the age of technology/the information age, (NOT the technology age).

We live in the modern age of technology. *(Don't say: We live in the modern technology age).*

We live in the information age. *(Don't say: We live in the ~~technology age~~).*

He didn't grow up in the age of technology. *(Don't say: He didn't grow up in the ~~technology age~~).*

We say developed society, (NOT ~~development/developmental~~ society).

We live in a well-developed society. *(Don't say: We live in a ~~development/developmental~~ society).*

People in developed societies seldom confront discrimination. *(Don't say: People in ~~development/developmental~~ societies seldom confront discrimination).*

We say …two years older than…, (NOT ~~older two years than~~).

He is two years older than I am. *(Don't say: He is ~~older two years than~~ I am).*

Her sisters is three years older than she is. *(Don't say: Her sisters is ~~older three years than~~ she is).*

We say six miles long, (NOT ~~long six miles~~).

The race was six miles long. *(Don't say: The race was ~~long six miles~~).*

This river is one hundred kilometers long. *(Don't say: This river is ~~long one hundred kilometers~~).*

We say 4 metres high, (NOT ~~high 4 metres~~).

The statue is 4 metres high. *(Don't say: The statue is ~~high 4 metres~~).*

The wall is six metres high. *(Don't say: The wall is ~~high six metres~~).*

We say eleven feet deep, (NOT ~~deep eleven feet~~).

The ditch is eleven feet deep. *(Don't say: The ditch is ~~deep eleven feet~~).*

The river is ten feet deep. *(Don't say: The river is ~~deep ten feet~~).*

Numbers must go before adjectives.

I'll need ten large pizzas for my birthday party. *(Don't say: I'll need ~~large ten pizzas~~ for my birthday party).*

May I have five small pieces of paper? *(Don't say: May I have ~~small five pieces~~ of paper?)*.

"First", "next" and "last" usually go before "one", "two", "three", "four" etc.

I want to rent the house for the first two weeks in May. *(Don't say: I want to rent the house for the ~~two first weeks~~ in May)*.

Tom will be staying with his relatives in New York for the next three weeks. *(Don't say: Tom will be staying with his relatives in New York for the ~~three next weeks~~)*.

She was sick for the last five days, but now she feels well. *(Don't say: She was sick for the ~~five last days~~, but now she feels well)*.

We use adverb + verb + object, (NOT ~~verb + adverb~~ + object).

I often eat vegetarian food. *(Don't say: I ~~eat often~~ vegetarian food)*.

I usually play football on Wednesday evenings. *(Don't say: I ~~play usually~~ football on Wednesday evenings)*.

We use verb + object + adverb, (NOT ~~verb + adverb~~ + object).

She plays the piano well. *(Don't say: She ~~plays well~~ the piano)*.

He speaks Japanese well. *(Don't say: He ~~speaks well~~ Japanese)*.

Adverbs of place usually go before adverbs of time.

He performed excellently at the interview yesterday. *(Don't say: He performed excellently ~~yesterday at the interview~~)*.

I worked hard at the office today. *(Don't say: I worked hard ~~today at the office~~)*.

We use be + always/usually/often/sometimes, etc., (NOT always/usually/often/sometimes ~~+ be~~).

He is always busy. *(Don't say: He ~~always is~~ busy)*.

He is usually straightforward and sincere. *(Don't say: He ~~usually is~~ straightforward and sincere)*.

She is often very talkative. *(Don't say: She often is very talkative).*

He is sometimes absent from school. *(Don't say: He sometimes is absent from school).*

Probably, certainly, definitely, clearly, obviously usually go before auxiliary verbs.

She probably thinks you're crazy! *(Don't say: She thinks probably you're crazy!).*

She certainly misses her children. *(Don't say: She misses certainly her children).*

He clearly heard the sound of bells. *(Don't say: He heard clearly the sound of bells).*

I definitely agree with you. *(Don't say: I agree definitely with you).*

I will definitely come late today. *(Don't say: I will come definitely late today).*

He obviously lied. *(Don't say: He lied obviously).*

She obviously missed something. *(Don't say: She missed obviously something).*

We use adverb + adjective, (NOT adjective + adjective).

It's extremely hot today. *(Don't say: It's extreme hot today).*

It's definitely wrong to stop him from seeing his parents. *(Don't say: It's definite wrong to stop him from seeing his parents).*

We use after all, (NOT finally) to say that something is contrary to what was expected.

It didn't rain after all. *(Don't say: It didn't rain finally).*

At first Peter said he would come to the party, but he's not going to come after all. *(Don't say: At first Peter said he would come to the party, but he's not going to come finally).*

We say she is twenty years old/of age. (NOT ...twenty years).

He is 19 years old. *(Don't say: He is 19 years).*

She is 21 years of age. *(Don't say: She is 21 years).*

We say be the same age as. (NOT ...be ~~at~~ the same age as...).

Tom is the same age as Mary. *(Don't say: Tom is ~~at~~ the same age as Mary).*

She's the same age as my sister. *(Don't say: She's ~~at~~ the same age as my sister).*

We say at the age of, (NOT ... ~~in~~ the age of ...).

He died at the age of 80. *(Don't say: He died ~~in~~ the age of 80).*

I graduated from college at the age of 22. *(Don't say: I graduated from college ~~in~~ the age of 22).*

We use like before a noun, (NOT ~~alike~~).

He is like his father. *(Don't say: He is ~~alike~~ his father).*

She is like her mom. *(Don't say: She is ~~alike~~ her mom).*

We say all students, (NOT all ~~of~~ students).

All students are being taught in the classroom. *(Don't say: All ~~of~~ students are being taught in the classroom).*

All people are having dinner at the restaurant. *(Don't say: All ~~of~~ people are having dinner at the restaurant).*

We use not all + plural noun + plural verb, (NOT not all + plural noun + ~~singular verb~~).

Not all students are lazy. *(Don't say: Not all students ~~is~~ lazy).*

Not all women are mothers. *(Don't say: Not all women ~~is~~ mothers).*

We say ...not only..., but...as well. Or...not only..., but....also.... (NOT ...not only...; but....~~either~~).

He not only sings, but he plays the guitar as well. *(Don't say: He not only sings, but he plays the guitar ~~either~~).*

He not only sings, but he also plays the guitar. *(Don't say: He not only sings, but* he also plays the guitar *either*).

We use though/although + clause, (NOT ~~despite/in spite of~~ + clause).

Although she doesn't like flying, he goes abroad on holiday. *(Don't say: ~~despite/in spite of~~ she doesn't like flying, he goes abroad on holiday).*

Although Mary is rich, she dresses quite simply. *(Don't say: ~~despite/in spite of~~ Mary is rich, she dresses quite simply).*

Although he smiled, he was angry. *(Don't say: ~~despite/in spite of~~ he smiled, he was angry).*

When we join two or more grammatically similar expressions, we usually put "and" before the last.

He likes tea, coffee and hot chocolate. *(Don't say: He likes tea, coffee, hot chocolate).*

We talked, played games and drank late until the night. *(Don't say: We talked, played games, drank late until the night).*

At night we talked, played chess and made a fire. *(Don't say: At night we talked, played chess, made a fire).*

We use fixed order bread and butter, (NOT ~~butter and bread~~).

I ate nothing but bread and butter. *(Don't say: I ate nothing but ~~butter and bread~~).*

She likes bread and butter. *(Don't say: She likes ~~butter and bread~~).*

We use fixed order young and pretty, (NOT ~~pretty and young~~).

She is young and pretty. *(Don't say: She is ~~pretty and young~~).*

Mary is young and pretty and warm-hearted. *(Don't say: Mary is ~~pretty and young~~ and warm-hearted).*

We use fixed order black and white, (NOT ~~white and black~~).

He has a dog that is black and white. *(Don't say: He has a dog that is ~~white and black~~).*

The most colorful thing in the world is black and white. *(Don't say: The most colorful thing in the world is ~~white and black~~).*

We use fixed order knife and fork, (NOT ~~fork and knife~~).

What are some foods you usually eat with a knife and fork? *(Don't say: What are some foods you usually eat with a ~~fork and knife~~).*

She doesn't know how to use knives and forks. *(Don't say: She doesn't know how to use ~~forks and knives~~).*

He sat down and ate his dinner with a knife and fork. *(Don't say: He sat down and ate his dinner with a ~~fork and knife~~).*

We say come and have a drink, (NOT ~~go~~ and have a drink).

Come and have a drink with us. *(Don't say: ~~Go~~ and have a drink with us).*

I'll come and have a drink with you but I must let Mary know. *(Don't say: He I'll ~~go~~ and have a drink with you but I must let Mary know).*

You're very welcome to come and have a drink at our bar and enjoy an extra show. *(Don't say: You're very welcome to ~~go~~ and have a drink at our bar and enjoy an extra show).*

Why don't you come and have dinner with us? *(Don't say: Why don't you ~~go~~ and have dinner with us?).*

We use another + singular countable nouns, (NOT another + ~~plural~~ countable nouns).

He's bought another house. *(Don't say: He's bought another ~~houses~~).*

Will you have another cup of tea? *(Don't say: Will you have another ~~cups~~ of tea?).*

May I have another piece of cake? *(Don't say: May I have another ~~pieces~~ of cake?).*

We use "no" to begin a sentence.

No cigarette is harmless. *(Don't say: ~~Not~~ any cigarette is harmless).*

No cigarette is allowed in the reading room. *(Don't say: ~~Not~~ cigarette is allowed in the reading room).*

No food is perfect. *(Don't say: ~~Not~~ food is perfect).*

No food is allowed to leave the cafeteria. *(Don't say: ~~Not~~ food is allowed to leave the cafeteria).*

We say an elephant, an apple, an orange, etc., (NOT ~~a~~ elephant, ~~a~~ apple, ~~a~~ orange).

We saw an elephant at the zoo. *(Don't say: We saw ~~a~~ elephant at the zoo).*

She wants an apple. *(Don't say: She wants ~~a~~ apple).*

I eat an apple every day. *(Don't say: I eat ~~a~~ apple every day).*

He gave his mother an orange in exchange for a piece of cake. *(Don't say: He gave his mother ~~a~~ orange in exchange for a piece of cake).*

We say an hour, (NOT ~~a~~ hour).

Give me an hour. *(Don't say: Give me ~~a~~ hour).*

I'll be back in an hour. *(Don't say: I'll be back in ~~a~~ hour).*

We say progress, (NOT ~~a~~ progress). Progress is uncountable.

He has made very good progress. (Don't say: He has made ~~a~~ very good progress).

We say weather, (NOT ~~a~~ weather). Weather is uncountable.

Did you have good weather on your trip? *(Don't say: Did you have ~~a~~ good weather on your trip?).*

If the weather is bad, I won't go out for a walk. *(Don't say: If ~~a~~ weather is bad, I won't go out for a walk).*

It is terrible weather today. *(Don't say: It is ~~a~~ terrible weather today).*

We use "the" with the names of musical instruments.

We say the guitar, the piano, the violin, (NOT ~~guitar, piano, violin~~).

Tom played the guitar and Mary played the piano. *(Don't say: Tom played the guitar and Mary played the piano).*

He likes to play the guitar. *(Don't say: He likes to ~~play guitar~~).*

Are you sure that Peter plays the violin well? *(Don't say: Are you sure that Peter ~~plays violin~~ well?).*

I can play the piano, the guitar and the violin. *(Don't say: I can ~~play piano, guitar and violin~~).*

We say "Do you like apples?", (NOT Do you like ~~apple~~?).

She likes butterflies because they are pretty. *(Don't say: She likes ~~butterfly~~ because they are pretty).*

I like cats. *(Don't say: I like ~~cat~~).*

We say what + a/an + adj + singular countable nouns, (NOT what + adj + singular countable nouns).

What a lovely house! *(Don't say: What lovely house!).*

What a big dog! *(Don't say: What big dog!).*

What a stupid man he is! *(Don't say: What stupid man he is!).*

We say as long as I have, (NOT as long as I ~~will~~ have).

I will learn English as long as I have time. *(Don't say: I will learn English as long as I ~~will~~ have time).*

I will study Japanese as long as I live in Japan. *(Don't say: I will study Japanese as long as I ~~will~~ live in Japan).*

I will go to London on holidays as long as I get the money. *(Don't say: I will go to London on holidays as long as I ~~will~~ get the money).*

We say as usual, (NOT as ~~usually~~).

Needless to say, Judy came late as usual. *(Don't say: Needless to say, Judy came* late *as usually*).

As usual, he was late. *(Don't say: As usually, he was late).*

We say ask someone for something, (NOT ask *someone something*).

He asked me for some money. *(Don't say: He asked me some money).*

She asked him for help. *(Don't say: She asked him help).*

He asked her for a loan. *(Don't say: He asked her a loan).*

We say ask someone to do something, (NOT ask someone *do/doing* something).

He asked me to lend him some money. *(Don't say: He asked me lend him some money).*

He asked her to marry him. *(Don't say: He asked her marry him).*

She asked me to show her the book. *(Don't say: She asked me show her the book).*

We say arrive in/at, (NOT ask arrive *to*).

I arrived in New York at 10:30 a.m. *(Don't say: I arrived to New York at 10:30 a.m).*

We arrived at the hotel and booked in. *(Don't say: We arrived to the hotel and booked in).*

We arrived at the harbor just as the boat was leaving. *(Don't say: We arrived to the harbor just as the boat was leaving).*

We say on the second floor, (NOT *in/at* the second floor).

My flat is on the second floor. *(Don't say: My flat is in/at the second floor).*

His office is on the second floor. *(Don't say: His office is in/at the second floor).*

We say give someone something back, (NOT give someone something *again*).

Give me my money back. (*Don't say: Give me my money ~~again~~*).

She gave him his book back. (*Don't say: She gave him his book ~~again~~*).

We say be one of the + plural nouns, (NOT be one of the + ~~singular nouns~~).

Venice is one of the most beautiful cities in Europe. (*Don't say: Venice is one of the most beautiful ~~city~~ in Europe*).

My father is one of the most important people in my life. (*Don't say: My father is one of the most important ~~person~~ in my life*).

We say we can both speak English, (NOT ~~both~~ we can speak English).

We can both learn from each other. (*Don't say: ~~Both we can~~ learn from each other*).

We can both drive cars. (*Don't say: ~~Both we can~~ drive cars*).

They can both be false. (*Don't say: ~~Both they can~~ be false*).

We use modal verbs + Vo.

He can speak English very well. (*Don't say: He ~~cans~~ speak English very well*).

She could read when she was three years old. (*Don't say: She could ~~to~~ read when she was three years old*).

Can you swim? (*Don't say: ~~Do you can~~ swim?*).

We use "may" to talk about the chances that something will happen, (NOT ~~can~~).

We may visit our grandparents in Sydney this year. (*Don't say: We ~~can~~ visit our grandparents in Sydney this year*).

I may pass the exam. (*Don't say: I ~~can~~ pass the exam*).

I may not have time to do it. (*Don't say: I ~~cannot~~ have time to do it*).

We say more and more beautiful, (NOT more ~~beautiful~~ and more beautiful).

She became more and more beautiful as she grew up. *(Don't say: She became more ~~beautiful~~ and more beautiful as she grew up)*.

He became more and more handsome as he grew older. *(Don't say: He became more ~~handsome~~ and more handsome as he grew older)*.

We use the + comparative expression + subject + verb.

The more he ate, the smarter he got. *(Don't say: The more he ate, ~~the more he got smarter~~.)*

The more books he read, the more he learned. *(Don't say: The more books he read, ~~he learned the more~~.)*

We say in the team, (NOT ~~of~~ the team).

He is the best player in the team. *(Don't say: He is the best player ~~of~~ the team)*.

She is the most talented person in the team. *(Don't say: She is the most talented person ~~of~~ the team)*.

CONCLUSION

Thank you again for downloading this book on " *"Common English Mistakes Explained With Examples: Over 600 Mistakes Almost Students Make and How To Avoid Them In Less Than 5 Minutes A."* and reading all the way to the end. I'm extremely grateful.

If you know of anyone else who may benefit from the useful over 600 mistakes almost students make and how to avoid them presented in this book, please help me inform them of this book. I would greatly appreciate it.

Finally, if you enjoyed this book and feel that it has added value to your work and study in any way, please take a couple of minutes to share your thoughts and post a REVIEW on Amazon. Your feedback will help me to continue to write the kind of Kindle books that helps you get results. Furthermore, if you write a simple REVIEW with positive words for this book on Amazon, you can help hundreds or perhaps thousands of other readers who may want to improve their English writing skills sounding like a native speaker. Like you, they worked hard for every penny they spend on books. With the information and recommendation you provide, they would be more likely to take action right away. We really look forward to reading your review.

Thanks again for your support and good luck!

If you enjoy my book, please write a POSITIVE REVIEW on amazon.

-- Rachel Mitchell --

CHECK OUT OTHER BOOKS

Go here to check out other related books that might interest you:

https://www.amazon.com/dp/B06W2P6S22

Marriage Heat: 7 Secrets Every Married Couple Should Know On How To Fix Intimacy Problems, Spice Up Marriage & Be Happy Forever

https://www.amazon.com/dp/B01ITSW8YU

Smart Kids Smart Money: The Ultimate Parent's Guide To Teaching
Kids About Earning, Saving, Giving, Spending And Investing Money
Wisely

https://www.amazon.com/dp/B01KEZVFU4

Legal Vocabulary In Use: Master 600+ Essential Legal Terms And Phrases Explained In 10 Minutes A Day

http://www.amazon.com/dp/B01L0FKXPU

Shortcut To Ielts Writing: The Ultimate Guide To Immediately Increase Your Ielts Writing Scores

http://www.amazon.com/dp/B01JV7EQGG

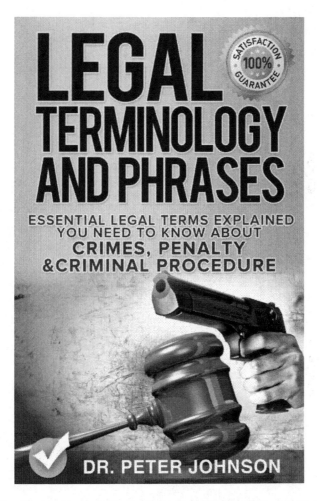

Legal Terminology And Phrases: Essential Legal Terms Explained You Need To Know About Crimes, Penalty And Criminal Procedure

http://www.amazon.com/dp/B01L5EB54Y

Productivity Secrets For Students: The Ultimate Guide To Improve
Your Mental Concentration, Kill Procrastination, Boost Memory And
Maximize Productivity In Study

http://www.amazon.com/dp/B01JS52UT6

Daughter of Strife: 7 Techniques On How To Win Back Your Stubborn Teenage Daughter

https://www.amazon.com/dp/B01HS5E3V6

Parenting Teens With Love And Logic: A Survival Guide To Overcoming The Barriers Of Adolescence About Dating, Sex And Substance Abuse

https://www.amazon.com/dp/B01JQUTNPM

Female Organism: The Best Oral Sex Ever To Give Her A Mind-Blowing Pleasure

https://www.amazon.com/dp/B01KIOVC18

GETTING OVER AN AFFAIR

100% SATISFACTION GUARANTEE

5 BIG SECRETS
EXPERTS WANT YOU TO KNOW ON HOW TO
DEAL WITH YOUR PARTNER'S INFIDELITY

JULIE ROSE

http://www.amazon.com/dp/B01J7G5IVS

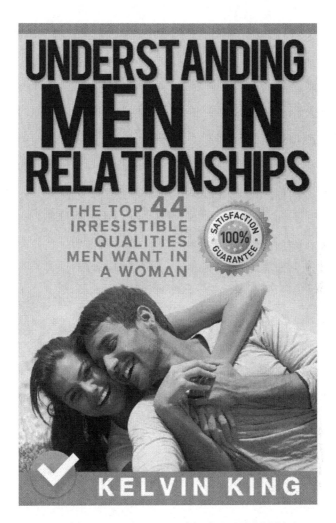

http://www.amazon.com/dp/B01K0ARNA4